Write Great Dialogue

How to write convincing dialogue, conversation and dialect in your fiction

Irving Weinman

First published in Great Britain in 2012 by Hodder Education. An Hachette UK company.

First published in US in 2012 by The McGraw-Hill Companies, Inc.

This edition published in 2019 by John Murray Learning

Paperback ISBN 9781473688513

Ebook ISBN 9781473688520

1

The publisher has used its best endeavours to ensure that any website addresses referred to in this book are correct and active at the time of going to press. However, the publisher and the author have no responsibility for the websites and can make no guarantee that a site will remain live or that the content will remain relevant, decent or appropriate.

The publisher has made every effort to mark as such all words which it believes to be trademarks. The publisher should also like to make it clear that the presence of a word in the book, whether marked or unmarked, in no way affects its legal status as a trademark.

Every reasonable effort has been made by the publisher to trace the copyright holders of material in this book. Any errors or omissions should be notified in writing to the publisher, who will endeavour to rectify the situation for any reprints and future editions.

Cover image © Shutterstock.com

Typeset by Cenveo® Publisher Services.

Printed and bound in Great Britain by CPI Group (UK) Ltd., Croydon, CR0 4YY.

John Murray Learning policy is to use papers that are natural, renewable and recyclable products and made from wood grown in sustainable forests. The logging and manufacturing processes are expected to conform to the environmental regulations of the country of origin.

Carmelite House
50 Victoria Embankment
London EC4Y 0DZ
www.hodder.co.uk

Also available as an ebook

Contents

About the Author

Among Irving Weinman's critically acclaimed novels are *Tailor's Dummy, Virgil's Ghost, Stealing Home* and *Wolf Tones*. He taught fiction writing in the United States and England, most recently a masterclass for the MA in Creative Writing and Authorship at Sussex University. He was founder-director of the Key West Writer's Workshop and a director of the Key West Seminar. Irving Weinman lived in Sussex with his wife, the poet Judith Kazantis. He passed away in 2015 and is survived by Judith and her daughter Miranda, his son and daughter in America, Michael and Zoe, as well as grandchildren.

ICON

 Focus point

 Key idea

 Write

Acknowledgements

The author thanks Chris Sykes for putting him in touch, and, as always, Judith for keeping him in touch. He also thanks Helen Rogers and the editorial staff at John Murray Learning. The author and the publisher would like to thank the authors and/ or publishers for permission to publish the following extracts from:

Auto da Fé (Die Blendung) ©Elias Canetti 1935, English translation © C.V. Wedgwood 1946, Penguin Books, 1973

MY OEDIPUS COMPLEX AND OTHER STORIES by Frank O'Connor (Penguin Books, 2005). Text copyright © Literary Executors of the Estate of Frank O'Connor, 1931, 1933, 1936, 1940, 1942, 1944, 1945, 1947, 1950, 1951, 1952, 1954, 1955, 1956, 1957, 1959, 1964, 1966. Reproduced by permission of Penguin Books Ltd.

"Men of Ireland" from CHEATING AT CANASTA by William Trevor (Viking 2007, Penguin Books 2008). Copyright © William Trevor, 2007. Reproduced by permission of Penguin Books Ltd.

Empire Falls © Richard Russo 2001, Vintage, 2002

The Stone Angel © Margaret Laurence 1964, Virago, 1986

Every reasonable effort has been made by the publisher to trace the copyright holders of material in this book. Any errors or omissions should be notified in writing to the publisher, who will endeavour to rectify the situation for any reprints and future editions.

Short, important introduction

On the first meeting of every fiction writing course and workshop I teach – from absolute beginners to published postgraduates – I say the same thing: 'This is my lecture on how to write and how not to write. It's my best lecture.'

After a pause, I say, 'This is the first part of the lecture – how to write.' I then take a pen and for a few seconds I write on a pad of paper. Then I pick up the pad of paper and say, 'It says, "This is how to write."'

After another pause (I'm hamming it up, I know) I say, 'This is the second part of the lecture – how not to write.' I pick up my pen, look down at the writing pad, scratch my head and look away from the pad. I look up at the ceiling. I purse my lips and furrow my forehead. I tilt my head back and narrow my eyes, still looking up at the ceiling. I make noises, 'uuhms' and 'aahs' of effort. I scratch my head again. Then I turn the still blank writing pad to the group and say, 'This is how not to write.' I add something about the muse or inspiration not coming at my command, coming only, if at all, when I'm actually writing.

'That's it,' I say, 'end of lecture.'

The whole performance has taken about four minutes. Then I add, 'Whatever else happens in this course, this is the best advice you'll hear from me.'

It's true. You learn to write by writing. You learn to write fiction by writing it. You learn to write narrative by writing it. And you learn to write dialogue by writing it. Yes, I do want you to buy this book, but this is the most important single piece of information I – or any other 'how to write' author – can give you. This is the bit that's most important.

Irving Weinman

1

An overview of dialogue

In this chapter you will learn:

- The basics of dialogue: what it is and how it functions
- How dialogue relates to other elements of fiction such as character and plot
- The various forms in which dialogue may occur
- Ways of moving into and out of dialogue
- About less frequent types of dialogue.

What is dialogue in fiction?

Dialogue in fiction is the written representation of speech between two or more people. Dialogue in real life is the speech between two or more people, what they say to each other. Because most real-life conversation is full of pauses, broken thoughts, repetitions and non-verbal sounds like 'uhm,' erm', and 'ahh' while thinking, writers would be crazy to put actual real-life dialogue into fiction. It would either bore readers or irritate them so much they'd stop reading.

Key idea

The trick or the craft or the art of writing good dialogue involves an imitation ('the written representation') of conversation that:
- keeps the story going
- reveals the characters
- is believable
- interests the readers.

These are the four characteristics of good dialogue.

Write

In my 'Short, important introduction' I promised that my best advice on 'how to write' is to write. Take no more than ten minutes to write one page (300 words) of dialogue between two characters. They don't know each other; they're meeting for the first time, and it's the opening of a piece of fiction. (Look briefly at the list of four characteristics of good dialogue above and then forget them and start writing. That's right, don't think about writing – just write!)

Another reason that conversation in fiction can't be exactly like conversation in life is that in life people often speak at the same time. Even if a writer made two parallel columns of speech to indicate simultaneous speech, it wouldn't work. The eye reads linearly. Though you can hear several words at once and make some sense of them, you simply can't read two things at once.

What does dialogue do?

One useful way to think about fiction is that it presents itself in two different ways: through **narration** and through **action** (also called scene). Contemporary readers and writers often refer to narration as the 'telling' element and to action or scene as the 'showing' element of fiction.

Focus point

Dialogue is action – an important part of how fiction 'shows' rather than 'tells'.

Much of human interaction occurs through speech. Even when the interaction is primarily physical – working, fighting, making love – it is typically accompanied by speech. Showing brings life and drama to fiction. Dialogue is a major element of showing. Here's how it works:

Case study: The start of the novel *Auto da Fé* by Elias Canetti

'What are you doing here, my little man?'

'Nothing.'

'Then why are you standing here?'

'Just because.'

'Can you read?'

'Oh, yes!'

'How old are you?'

'Nine and a bit.'

'Which would you prefer, a piece of chocolate or a book?'

'A book.'

'Indeed? Splendid! So that's your reason for standing here?'

'Yes.'

'Why didn't you say so before?'

'Father scolds me.'

'Oh. And who is your father?'

'Franz Metzger.'

'Would you like to travel to a foreign country?'

'Yes. To India. They have tigers there.'

'And where else?'

'To China. They've got a huge wall there.'

'You'd like to scramble over it, wouldn't you?'

'It's much too thick and too high. Nobody can get over it. That's why they built it.'

'What a lot you know! You must have read a great deal already?'

'Yes. I read all the time. Father takes my books away. I'd like to go to a Chinese school. They have forty thousand letters in their alphabet. You couldn't get them all into one book.'

'That's only what you think.'

***

If we check this against the four characteristics of good dialogue, we find first that, as the opening of a novel, it gets the story going. Beginnings give the reader some sense of the *who, where* and *when* (character, setting, time) of the story. This is sometimes called the 'opening exposition'. Here, there's an adult – a man, we think – and a child. The man strikes up the conversation. The boy, at first reluctant, responds to the question about reading. From then on, the questions and answers form a seemingly logical, natural sequence. In other words, it becomes a conversation. It's obviously taking place outside, and there's even a clue that it occurs in front of a bookshop ('A book?' ... 'So that's your reason for standing here?') The German name, Franz Metzger, could indicate national location. And this sense of place, of a street, indicates it's taking place not 'once upon a time' but in a relatively modern, historical time.

Second, this dialogue begins to reveal character. It tells us that the boy is at first wary of the man and his questions, and then that he likes reading enough to respond to a question about reading, and that he has a father who disapproves of his interest in reading (partly explaining the boy's initial silence). As for the man, his motives for starting up the conversation may be innocent or sinister, but he clearly approves of the boy liking to read, and his delight in the boy's knowledge of China and Chinese indicates his own knowledge and interests.

The dialogue is definitely not an everyday conversation between an adult and child in a street, but it is made believable – the third characteristic of good dialogue – in several ways. There is the boy's typical reluctance to strike up conversation with an apparent stranger (he's doing 'Nothing' standing here; he's here 'Just because'). The dialogue also allows for the sense of natural digression common to real speech: the boy first speaks of wanting to go to India because 'They have tigers there' before speaking about China.

Fourth and finally, the dialogue interests us by moving so quickly from 'Nothing' and 'Just because' to a nine-year-old's discussion of 'forty thousand letters' in the Chinese alphabet. And the boy's mistake about the impossibility of books based on such an alphabet is amusing because it's so logical. In fact, the more we think of this conversation, the stranger it is. This intrigues us. We want to know more. If you don't know the book, a few lines further on, the dialogue has a shocking twist. (If you don't know the book, you might want to read it. It's one of the masterpieces of twentieth-century fiction.)

Where do writers find dialogue?

In Molière's play *Le Bourgeois Gentilhomme* ('The Would-be Gentleman'), a rich idiot is amazed to learn from a teacher he's hired that he's been speaking prose all his life. Writers, even beginning writers, have been speaking dialogue all their lives.

Focus point

Your first and best source of dialogue is your own speech.

As a writer, you draw on your lifelong practice of dialogue in creating your characters' dialogue. You speak in a range of emotions – anger, fear, love, loathing, joy and repulsion. You speak in a range of moods – reflective, exuberant, bored, ironic and earnest. You use a variety of levels of speech – formal and informal, standard and slang, curses and expletives you haven't deleted. Your speech includes a mix of jargons reflecting your interests – baking, banking, baseball, garage bands, gardening, plumbing and physics.

And you haven't had to give your speech a second thought. Until now. Now, as a writer trying to represent people speaking in a story, your own speech is your source, the absolute spring of your imagination.

It merely takes some practice, this sitting back and listening to the conversations in your head. And the practice it takes is writing, writing it out on the page, writing and (later) reading it over to hear what it sounds like. So you're the main source of the dialogue you write, but you're not the only source.

- **The talk of others** You've listened to other people talking all your life. As a writer, you become more aware of *how* others speak – how they emphasize some words, repeat words or phrases, how their voices sound low or piping, rough or syrupy, hesitant, insistent, or questioning even when they're not asking questions. Do they speak in a fast, flat, emotionless way? Do they chuckle when saying nothing funny?

- **The fiction of others** All the novels and stories you read are source books for dialogue. Of course, you don't copy the dialogue, but you look closely to see what makes you think this or that is really good, really 'gets' the tone, the character, the mood. By the way, reading like this, like a writer, makes reading more, not less, enjoyable. Recently, I was moving some books around and I opened one I'd read before at a random page and read:

'I could use the extra scratch,' Max said, falling in step and causing Miles to make a mental note to keep an eye on him tonight. His father hated work but loved crowds, probably because chaos created many more opportunities than order.

'Put on a clean shirt before you go out front,' Miles reminded him.

'I've worked here before, you know.'

'And an apron,' Miles said. 'And wash your hands.'

'Wash my hands so I can bus dirty dishes?'

That word 'scratch' caught me. I hadn't heard it in at least 20 years. It was just the word an ageing, feckless hippie would use instead of 'money'. (The book was Richard Russo's *Empire Falls*. Russo writes very, very good dialogue.)

- **Radio and television** These media present written dialogue, as in plays and sitcoms; half-memorized 'real' speech, as in interviews with politicians or newspaper proprietors, and the more spontaneous conversations sometimes found in chat shows and on-the-spot interviews with people in the street. They can provide good examples of people trying to turn a dialogue into a monologue, interruptions of dialogue and people insistent on speaking over, under and through the speech of other people, while the presenter's attempts to bring order to the discussion merely adds to the cacophony.

- **Plays** Plays are meant to be performed, and while you can read a play as 'pure' dialogue, with a few stage directions, the experience of being at a play involves you experiencing the physicality of the actors, their facial and bodily expressions, their actions. Then there's the set and the properties, and lighting and sound effects – the spectacle as well as the speech. The actors speak expressively, making real the playwright's intentions. And you, the writer of fiction, have none of this going for you: everything you do has to arise from words on the page. Nevertheless, you can sharpen your ears for the nuances of dialogue – its rhythms (which include its silences, stops and starts), its slight shifts of tone and its various levels of irony – by attending and reading plays.

- **Movies** Movies, in general, should be regarded as stories told visually. Of course, there are movies with good dialogue, but much of the emotional significance of dialogue resides in what you are seeing as the dialogue occurs. Visual movements from close-up to long shot, from speaker to listener, and from actor (character) to object or landscape during speech, are elements of film craft unavailable to the writer. Nor does the writer have a musical score to help direct the reader's emotions. Although fiction has incorporated a number of cinematic techniques, these, like the jump-cut, for example, generally belong to narration, rather than to dialogue. Still, you need to follow your interest in dialogue even into the cinema.

Focus point

Keep your ears open for dialogue wherever you hear or read it.

How is dialogue presented on the page?

Standard presentations of dialogue are indicated visually and by supporting narrative:

- **Visual presentations** Direct speech is generally put in quotation marks. Contemporary practice is to use single marks to indicate the beginning and end of direct speech. Double marks are reserved for quotes within direct speech. The second visual marker of direct speech is to begin a new paragraph to indicate a change of speaker. Does every writer use these? No, but most do, and unless you are adding something to your dialogue by doing away with them, you should use them. They make clear what is taking place on the page.
- **Supporting narrative** This is used for:
  o identifying the speaker
  o indicating speech tone
  o describing the speaker's or listener's facial expression
  o describing the speaker's or listener's body expression and action

o describing the setting

o stating the unspoken thoughts and feelings

o narrator's reflections or observations.

Let's look at each of these uses in turn.

IDENTIFYING THE SPEAKER

This is the 'she said' or 'the boy said' or 'Max said' accompanying the dialogue.

INDICATING SPEECH TONE

This literally or figuratively states the emotion of the dialogue.

'I never could,' Amy said mournfully.

'I never could,' Amy said. Her words seemed to echo in the fading light.

In the first example the narrative is literal, in the second, figurative.

DESCRIBING THE SPEAKER'S OR LISTENER'S FACIAL EXPRESSION

This explains the meaning of the dialogue by focusing on facial expression. It may be direct or ironic.

'I never could,' Amy said, her eyes dropping, her mouth turning down.

'I never could,' Amy said, with a slightly challenging smile.

The first example directly describes sad facial expression. In the second, the narrative would be ironic if in context the reader (or character listening) expected a sad expression.

The irony might be revealing a self-protective attitude, or pride, or both at once.

DESCRIBING THE SPEAKER'S OR LISTENER'S BODY EXPRESSION AND ACTION

Body expression can function like facial expression. It is often less consciously controlled than facial expression. Like facial expression, it can be used directly or ironically.

'I never could,' Amy said mournfully.

Harry leaned forward and reached out his hand.

'I never could,' Amy said mournfully.

Harry leaned forward, began to reach out his hand, and drew it back. 'No, Amy,' he said, 'I'm not falling for it, this time.'

In the second example, Harry's body response is the physical version of the spoken rejection that follows.

DESCRIBING THE SETTING

The writer may choose to break into the dialogue to give a sense of place, time, or other aspects of location.

'I never could,' said Amy mournfully. The dark furniture of Harry's study disturbed her. It felt so completely inherited.

'I never could,' said Amy mournfully. The white furniture of Harry's bright, neat study seemed cold to her, inhuman.

In the first example, the setting works with the tone of the dialogue. In the second, it ironically works against it.

STATING THE UNSPOKEN THOUGHTS AND FEELINGS

These can augment the dialogue by adding emotions, qualifications, or contradictions.

'I never could,' Amy said mournfully. She heard herself appealing for sympathy she didn't really want from Harry.

'I never could,' Amy said mournfully. Of course she could, but it was important that Harry didn't know it. It was important, she found herself thinking, that Harry kept thinking of her as a dull, self-pitying girl.

The interjections of thoughts and feelings into dialogue can add depth to the scene, creating layers of meaning below the surface of the words actually spoken.

NARRATOR'S REFLECTIONS OR OBSERVATIONS

A typical feature in nineteenth-century dialogue, these faded from use in twentieth-century modernism. Some contemporary writers use such interventions, either in a postmodern, meta-fictional way or without such self-consciousness.

'I never could,' said Amy mournfully. Amy was trying it on. She often tried on moods and attitudes to see what would happen.

'I never could,' said Amy mournfully. At least, she thought it sounded mournful. For all I know, it may have sounded silly.

In the first example, the writing stays within a representation of realism. In the second, the interjection breaks out of the convention of 'knowing' what a character was 'actually' doing.

How much supporting narrative should a writer use in dialogue?

Short answer: Enough.

Longer answer: Enough.

In other words, there is no answer before the fact. In the first two examples given earlier, the dialogue from *Auto da Fé* has no supporting narrative, and the dialogue from *Empire Falls* has more supporting narrative than direct speech. Both are effective. Moreover, each of the novels uses a range of supporting narrative in scenes of dialogue. Generally, most novels and short stories use a mix of length and type of supporting narrative in dialogue. There are some writers, however, whose fiction is characterized by the dominance of dialogue or of narrative. The novels of Ivy Compton-Burnett and Henry Green are substantially dialogue. The short stories of Jorge Luis Borges are mostly narrative.

Write

First, write one page (around 300 words) of dialogue between two people who know each other using no supporting narrative. Then write the same dialogue using about the same amount of supporting narrative as direct speech (around 600 words in total).

When you finish, consider the differences between the two versions. What are the strengths of each? What are the weaknesses?

How does dialogue represent character?

Narration can describe character at length and in detail, but it can't *show* character. Character is shown through action, and dialogue is a major form of action in fiction. Dialogue shows character; it brings character to life on the page.

Since what the characters do and say makes up the story – makes up what happens in fiction – characters cannot literally be separated from plot. But we nevertheless do this for the purpose of understanding key components of creating a fictional character's dialogue.

Of course, what is said always depends on the speaker's intention in speaking and on her/his response to the speech of other characters. Additionally, writers have to be aware of the links between these four basic components of dialogue and other speech determinants such as: emotion, age, ethnicity, gender, local or regional speech, education, class, occupation, and mental and physical health.

The basic components take on meaning only in context. 'Ivan go,' if spoken by an 18-month-old infant might mean that he, Ivan, wants to go out to play with his older sister. A 38-yearold immigrant might say 'Ivan go,' meaning he's going to bring up the equipment left downstairs. Both speakers are new to the language and have a limited vocabulary. Though their basic grammar (subject–verb order) is correct, their speech lacks the coherence of an older child saying 'I want to go out to play with Susie,' or of a more fluent immigrant saying 'I'll get it.' Nevertheless, both speakers will be understood in the context of the scene in which they speak.

Habits of speech can help characterize dialogue. Most often, a little goes a long way:

'How are you feeling this morning?' the nurse asked.

'Well, young feller, I'll tell you: not too good.'

'I'm sorry to hear that. I'm sure you'll feel better after your wash.'

'Well, young feller, I'll tell you: I don't think so.'

'Let's see. OK?'

'Well, young feller, I'll tell you: I already know.'

This is someone with a linguistic nervous tic. Unless this is the case for the character, a shorter repeated phrase, like 'young feller', and leaving it out of some of the speeches, will communicate the speech habit without forcing the readers to stop listening to the dialogue as they read because of the tiresome repetition. The edited dialogue might go like this:

'How are you feeling this morning?' the nurse asked.

'Well, young feller, not too good.'

'I'm sorry to hear that. I'm sure you'll feel better after your wash.'

'I don't think so.'

'Let's see. OK?'

'If you say so, young feller.'

How does dialogue in narrative differ from narrative in dialogue?

Dialogue in narrative refers to short pieces of dialogue within a longer narrative section.

On her way to the interview, Maggie tried to focus on her good working relation with Jessica, who was, after all, a good boss. She knew when to give you direction and when to let you get on with it. She was accessible and she really knew the marketing end of the business. Yet Maggie kept remembering that scene with Kate rushing from Jessica's office and Jessica saying in a quiet, unemotional voice, 'I have no time for snivelers.' Maggie really had to stop thinking about it.

Here, the little bit of dialogue not only shows Maggie's current tension, it also sets up the tension for the forthcoming interview scene.

Yet Maggie kept remembering that scene. Jessica's door had opened and Kate rushed out.

'Hi, Kate. In a hurry?'

Kate turned, red-faced. 'Yes, to get away from here. And I don't mean you.'

'Sorry,' Maggie said, wondering what had happened.

'Come in,' Jessica called from her desk.

Maggie said, 'Good morning,' trying to keep the embarrassment from her voice.

'Good morning. How's the plan coming?'

Maggie lifted the folder. 'Good. I've finished a draft of the outline.'

Jessica said, 'Excellent.' She stood and said, 'Sorry about Kate. I'm afraid I have no time for snivelers.'

Maggie nodded, too shocked to find a reply.

This is no longer a short piece of dialogue in the narrative. It's a scene on its own, an example of a scene in flashback, developed out of the narrative. The writer might start with this and in revising might reduce it to the first example of the one short dialogue statement. In this way, the writing could move into the interview scene (Maggie's possible promotion?) without stopping for the relatively humdrum scene above.

Common sense determines whether the dialogue is part of the narrative or is developed enough to be a scene of its own:

> Jack made his way across the crowded room towards his cousin. He always felt he had a lot to say to his cousin, yet when Larry saw him, flashed his grand smile and said, 'Jack! How's tricks?' he found himself at a loss for words. He had no 'tricks', didn't want to talk about 'tricks' at all.

As above, there's generally no problem identifying dialogue in narration. At its best, the bit of dialogue enlivens the narrative, reveals character (here it reveals more about Jack than about Larry) and develops the story.

Write

Taking the 600-word dialogue with supporting narration piece you've written in the last exercise, turn it into one paragraph of narration in which there is one or, at most, two short sentences of dialogue. Try to make the dialogue in your narrative important to the tone, meaning and characterization of your original piece.

How else does dialogue appear in fiction?

In addition to dialogue in scene and in narrative, dialogue occurs in a range of other representations in fiction:

- **In monologue** For clarity, first-person narration/point of view is not considered monologue, although the story-teller's personalized voice is monologue. Monologue usually refers to a character's long speech – paragraphs to pages long. The character is narrating within the overall narration, and part of this can be short bits of dialogue or an entire dialogue scene.
- **In thoughts** Thoughts can be represented in narration within scenes or in narrative sections of fiction. Dialogue can occur within the thought. The last example – 'Jack! How's

tricks?' – was within a thought during narrative. It might also have taken place during a scene of dialogue and supporting narration, as here:

> Twisting through the crowd, Jack found Jill Conroy.
>
> 'Here we are, Jack and Jill again,' she said. This was her usual greeting.
>
> 'We certainly are,' he said, looking over her head to where his cousin Larry was holding court in a corner.
>
> Jill came close and said in a mock whisper, 'Don't you think these sorts of affairs are death to any real conversation?'
>
> Jack nodded. 'Certainly.' He thought of all the things he wanted to say to his cousin.
>
> Yet he knew that if he went over to him, Larry would flash his grand smile, say, 'Jack! How's tricks?' and leave him speechless. He didn't have 'tricks'. He didn't want to talk about 'tricks'.

- **In letters, diaries, telephone conversations, voice messages, emails, texts, social networks and composites** All of these are forms of written and spoken speech that can be represented in fiction. (The written forms can be closer to the real thing than representations of spoken language.) All can include dialogue.
- **Letters** Some of the early examples of modern fiction are the eighteenth-century letter novels (epistolary novels). These are composed entirely of letters from the main character to others, or between two main characters, or between a series of characters. Within the letters, characters write the dialogue between themselves and others or dialogue overheard or reported to them.
- **Diaries** Diaries have been represented in English language fiction since the seventeenth century (Daniel Defoe, *A Journal of the Plague Year*). They continue to be part or the entire structure of novels and shorter fiction up to the present, and they can include dialogue as the 'record' of what occurred on a certain date. They occur less frequently today – probably because fewer people keep diaries.
- **Telephone conversations** These came into fiction as telephones began to be used in homes and offices. Part of the potential for characterization in telephone dialogue is in the difference between the way a person may speak over the telephone rather than face to face. The disembodied voice can be a powerful driver of characterization both in the speaker and the listener.

- **Voice messages** Appearing in fiction as the technology came into use, voice messages are, strictly, monologues. They can be constructed as dialogues between characters in which neither party can interrupt.
- **Emails and text formats** Emails have substantially replaced written letters. In my experience, very few contain dialogue, but the possibility is there. Texts and social networking can be thought of as the twenty-first-century versions of telegrams. The concision they impose can produce creative solutions that produce individuated voices.
- **Composites** Twenty-first-century century realism, as well as fantasy, can use a combination of characters' speaking voices and writing texts in developing character and presenting narrative. Such composites can vary and extend the single, overarching narrator and point of view.

Write

Take the paragraph you wrote in the last exercise and rewrite it as if you were speaking over the phone. Then take that phone talk and turn it into an email of the sort you would send. Finally, make it an electronic text message of no more than 140 characters.

What is the relation between dialogue and indirect speech?

Everyone remembers this sort of example from school:

Roberta said she was only borrowing the pen.

Roberta said, 'I was only borrowing the pen.'

The first statement is not dialogue (not direct quotation) because Roberta did not say 'she'. What Roberta did say is dialogue directly quoted in the second statement.

The fact that the difference between the indirect speech and the statement of dialogue is so small is an indication of how easily indirect speech can slip into dialogue and back out again.

Roberta said she was only borrowing the pen. She wasn't going to keep it. It wasn't the kind of pen she'd keep. 'I mean, I'm going to steal a pen; it sure's gonna be a lot more cool than that clear plastic mess of yours with chew marks all over it.' She said that anyhow she didn't steal pens.

The writer is able to bring Roberta to life by letting readers hear her speak. Once this happens, the final statement of indirect speech seems more like dialogue, is more lifelike, because the readers now have Roberta's voice in their minds.

The movement or transition between direct and indirect speech offers the writer important ways to mix narrative and dialogue and to vary the pace of the writing.

How does dialogue represent different elements of speech?

FOREIGN SPEECH

Writers represent foreign speech in a number of ways.

- In the original with no explanation:

    Jean said, '"Si Dieu n'existait pas, il faudrait l'inventer."'

    Sylvie said, 'I always know you've lost the argument when you begin quoting Voltaire.'

- In the original with a translation/explanation in the dialogue:

    Jean said, '"Si Dieu n'existait pas, il faudrait l'inventer."'

    Sylvie said, 'I always know you've lost the argument when you begin quoting Voltaire.'

    'What does it mean?' Bill asked.

    Sylvie said, 'It means: If God didn't exist it would be necessary to invent him.'

- In the original with a translation in the narrative:

    Jean said, '"Si Dieu n'existait pas, il faudrait l'inventer."'

    Hearing "If God did not exist, it would be necessary to invent him," Sylvie said, 'I always know you've lost the argument when you begin quoting Voltaire.'

- In a translation that indicates a foreigner speaking English:

    Jean said, 'If God was not there, it would require – you say "require?" – that he must be invented.'

    Sylvie said, 'I always know you've lost the argument when you begin quoting Voltaire.'

- In an un-idiomatic, literally translated English indicating the dialogue is spoken in another language:

    Jean said, 'If God existed not, it would be required to invent him.'

COLLOQUIAL PRONUNCIATIONS

In the earlier example of direct speech within indirect speech (dialogue within narrative) you read:

'I mean, I'm gonna steal a pen, it sure's gonna be a lot more cool than that clear plastic mess of yours with chew marks all over it.'

Readers will have no problem identifying 'gonna' as the colloquial pronunciation of 'going to.' This and many other representations of contractions, elisions and regional variants in pronunciation have become standardized in spelling over time. But writers are careful with their own one-off spellings of pronunciation, since they can easily be misread and misunderstood. There's no point of making any word more difficult than need be for the readers.

SPEECH ACCENTS

Foreign and regional accents can be represented in dialogue; the guidelines above for colloquial speech apply. But less is much better than too much, and the writer has to take care not to fall into clichés of representation.

Clint said, 'Ah'm warnin you, Kurt and Pierre, you jest ain't gonna make it goin thataway. You heah?'

'I vill not do dis dat you say,' Kurt replied.

Pierre said, 'On zee ozer hand, I weel take zees advice.'

This is a minefield of clichéd foreign accents. As a serious attempt it's disastrous. No reader would keep moving forward through such dialogue.

INTERRUPTIONS

Dialogue represents interruptions through conventions of punctuation, continuation of interrupted speech after the interruption(s) and partial repetitions. Supporting narrative is also used.

Janet said, 'Greece should never have been in the euro currency. The drachma –'

'It's not a question of the drachma,' Don put in.

'The drachma was too weak a currency com –'

'It was the Greek political patronage system, not the currency.'

'Compared to the euro to have a chance, suddenly having to be part –'

'But that's what I'm saying,' Don's voice rose over hers.

'They were forced to be overvalued, and their essential lack of a tax base –'

'No,' she said, 'to be part of a currency pulled them into a central banking system –'

And so forth.

MULTIPLE SPEECH

Though two or more people speaking simultaneously is literally impossible to read, an impression of multiple speech can be given through selective identification of speakers, disconnects between statements, and narrative information. This works best with short statements from each speaker.

Zoe said, 'Debbie should leave him. Phil's a rat.'

Then everybody began to talk at once.

'What should he do with a drunk like her?'

'How do you know what Phil's gone through?'

'She's not a drunk.'

'She does drugs, too.'

'Have some sympathy. She's the mother of his –'

'And what sort of father runs out –'

'Counselling was –'

'Needs help, not –'

Then Zoe called, 'Hey, Debbie girl!' and everyone shut up and turned toward the door.

CROWDS

The talk of larger crowds is represented in ways similar to multiple speech. The disconnections over larger physical spaces generally require more narrative description. The purpose of the crowd – political rally or religious gathering, street riot or baseball game – provides subject linkage for the bits of dialogue. Crowd talk is often presented in third-person omniscient narration. But limited point of view is also used. For instance, the character through whom the reader hears the voices in the crowd can be moving through it, or the crowd can be moving past the character.

 Key idea

Dialogue can represent many forms of speech in many different situations.

What are the paradoxes of dialogue?

One paradox is that dialogue can consist of two (or more) people supposedly speaking with each other without one or both really listening to each other. This is not the same as a series of monologues, because what each person says is in some way conditioned by their 'knowing' what the other is saying, despite not listening. The 'knowing' can be an incomplete or false idea of what the other is actually saying.

A second paradox is that writers can use their characters' dialogue to gain further critical insights into character and plot.

In other words, the characters, if properly listened to, can teach their writer to do better.

These paradoxes will be discussed towards the end of the book.

Focus points

Chapter 1 was an overview of the book to come. Its main ideas are summarized in the following five points:

- Good dialogue has four basic characteristics. First, good dialogue keeps the story going; dialogue is never an interruption of the story. It's part of the story's central action. It develops all aspects of the plot. Second, good dialogue reveals character. It shows who the characters are (not tells, shows). What a person says, whether true or false, whether reserved or extroverted, is an expression of character in action. Third, to be good, dialogue has to be believable. No matter how odd the character or how unusual her or his way of speaking, the reader has to be able to accept it. This means the reader believes it's possible enough in the context of the novel or story not to think it impossible or improbable. Fourth, good dialogue has to be interesting. This is obvious and maybe goes without saying, but not in a book about how to write dialogue.
- Dialogue is an important part of the action of a novel. The action directly *shows* the reader people and experiences rather than just telling them. Much of the interpersonal action of most people's lives is in conversation. Even when the action between people is more physical, dialogue plays a significant role.

- Your own speech is your first and best source for your characters' dialogue. You put yourself in your characters' shoes, see through their points of view, and you write this from out of your own experience of language. Central to that experience is your own use of language. You also rely on the speech you've heard and the speech you've read. All of this experience of language is modified in writing by your understanding of your characters' linguistic background, education and temperament. Finally, the context of the scene you're writing provides guidelines to what your characters say and how they say it.
- It's important to understand the role supporting narrative can play in any scene without having it overwhelm the dialogue. This means you're using the narration for clarity (who's speaking), for significant physical description (facial and bodily expression, physical action, and description of relevant objects, light, weather, background sounds, etc.). This also means not depending on the supporting narrative to explain the dialogue's literal or figurative meanings nor to substitute for the emotions which should be inherent to the speech.
- Finally, dialogue can be used in a wide range of formats (telephone, letters, emails, texts, etc.). Dialogue can also be used within narrative writing to exemplify and bring narration to life by having the character's voice 'appear' for emphasis and variety.

Next step

Chapter 2 moves on to a closer look at, and a more detailed study of, how your characters show who they are through dialogue.

2

Character in dialogue

In this chapter you will learn:
- How to build a character's voice
- How to create different voices for different characters
- About 'hearing' your characters' speech
- How to avoid dialogue stereotypes in age and gender.

The fiction you write is the product of your experiences, though you may not have literally experienced the story you tell nor the characters who enact it. What this means is that your writing comes from how you observe, conceive and imagine life is or could or should be.

It follows that your characters have this basis and that the language you have them speak comes out of your understanding of speech. This, in turn, means that your own practice of speech and your observation of speech (listening, watching and reading) and your imagining of speech produce your dialogue.

Part of your decision of what to write as dialogue is very rational. It answers the question: What information is to be communicated by speech between the characters in the scene? Another part is doubly irrational. First, it involves the emotional meanings you intend for the characters in the scene. Second, it involves the emotional meanings or understanding you intend the scene to give your readers, which may be different from the characters' understanding.

But these choices, your choices, also arise from your own affinities and antipathies in considering characters who are of your making but who are not you.

 Key idea

Writers create dialogue from their own speaking, listening and reading experience.

How can a writer build a character's voice?

You've read my repeated insistence that dialogue come first and foremost from your own speech, that it also comes from the speech and voices of others you've experienced, and that it also comes from the dialogue you've read and heard, and at times also watched, in books, plays, movies, radio, television and online. All very true, yet as you the writer face the empty page or blank screen, how are you supposed to come up with your character's voice?

 Key idea

Voice is not only what is said but how a character says it, what it sounds like.

Focus point

If voices don't come easily, you can get help by listing aspects
of your character's current life and background.

A writer's character notes might look like this (with a lot of crossing
out of first tries, etc.):

Name: George Chambers

Age: 53

Work: advertising copywriter, successful; lives in Islington,
London

Background: born Manchester

Parents: mother: Phyllis, history lecturer (18th-c. social history)
at Manchester Uni; father: Steven, head teacher state primary
school; both lifelong Labour Party; Steven died 2003; mother
living, retired.

Education: Manchester Grammar, Leeds Uni (English 1st class
honours)

Politics: says Lib Dem, privately votes Conservative

Newspapers: home – *Guardian*, work – *The Times, The Financial
Times, The Sun*

Appearance: 6ft, lean build – ran 400 meters at uni, sandy-
haired, white at temples; good-looking in an obvious way

Exercise: walks with Maeve (wife), jogs on own, watches
daughter Eileen (15) ride, though he doesn't like horses

Drink, etc.: drinks at working lunches and at pub/wine bar after
work, drinks moderately at home; smoked marijuana at uni; now
strongly disapproves of any rec. drugs; non-smoker, tends to be
environmentally green; has done successful green campaigns for
major polluters

Speech: speaks quickly, with wit, sometimes with cruel twist;
funny, intelligent (superficially?), rarely at loss for words

Given the character's background, education and work, the writer
was able to 'hear' George's voice. It's possible from these notes that
whatever Mancunian accent George had in school is now gone into a
standard, educated south of England accent. It might be, considering
his parents, that there was no local accent in their home. If so, given
these notes, you could expect that George as a schoolboy and at
university would have slid into whatever the dominant accent of the

group he hung out with or aspired to. Perhaps this might give the writer the idea that George could break into 'Mancunian' to show he's just one of the boys, if need be, or maybe in times of real stress, etc.

Note how making character notes on one (main) character starts to bring in ideas about other characters (parents, wife, child). And brief notes on these others can begin to suggest possible characteristics of their speech/voices. Even those merely given names – Maeve and Eileen – suggest possibilities such as an Irish background.

Why has the writer chosen to add George's track event in these notes? Though I wrote it, I don't know. It's one of the shorter, faster track events. Was the writer already thinking of 'quick-talking' ad men? Did this contribute to hearing George as 'speaks quickly'? Would this writer have given George another track event, say, the 10k or the marathon, had he been a philosopher or a psychoanalyst? This writer may have; another may not.

What's certain, however, is that all writers don't need character notes. A large-scale novel probably has its writer, at some point in the early drafts, jotting down a list or two, if only to keep track of a large cast of characters and their relationships.

 Write

> Make character notes for someone who might be in a piece of fiction you write. Make the notes on the character's speech/voice come last, based on all the other notes.

Following are extracts from two scenes of dialogue. In each scene a young person is warned by a parent figure about the dangers of a relationship.

Case study: Character and drama

Extract 1 – from *Madame Sousatzka*, by Bernice Rubens

...He stopped playing.

'I've learned so much with her, Momma,' he said. 'D'you know, I never understood the piano before I went to her.'

'How much is it to understand before you give a concert? Nine months it is already. So many pieces. So much practising. What for, I'm asking.'

'You're impatient, Momma. She says I can give a concert when I'm ready.'

'When he's ready, when he's ready.' Mrs. Crominski was exasperated. "For me, you're ready. Marcus,' she said solemnly, 'I'm thinking you should leave her.'

'No!' Marcus shouted. It wasn't only Madam Sousatzka he would have to leave. It was Uncle, Jenny and Cordle. It was a whole way of life he would have to surrender. 'No, I'm not leaving her,' he said defiantly. 'She's the best teacher in London, Momma,' he begged. 'I don't want to leave her.

'So all your life you'll stay with Madame Sousatzka. A beard you'll grow there and still you're not ready. Is no good, Marcus. Money I'm not wasting. That I know. But time. Time. Next week I'll go and tell her. Is time you're wasting and a hump you're growing. Yes, a hump. I don't care what she calls it. Is still there. Have you ever heard such a thing! A boy should go for piano lessons and a hump he gets. Next Friday, I'll tell her, and this time, believe me, I'm not listening to any nonsense.'

'I'll tell her,' said Marcus. "I'll tell her today. There you are. I'll tell her at today's lesson. Then you don't have to come and see her.'

'Today in any case you can tell her. Next Friday, I go. Tell her I come. Next Friday, tell her, you should be ready for a concert.'

Extract 2 – from *Love Medicine*, by Louise Erdrich

Still, in going to Moses Pillager I didn't mean to upset so many people. At first, I only wanted to disturb old Rushes Bear.

'Tell me about Moses,' I asked Nanapush.

He studied my face, his head to one side, and saw my intentions as clearly as if I had stated them.

'What do you want with Moses?' Rushes Bear was instantly alert. 'Stay away from that *djessikid*!'

Nanapush agreed that I should not disturb Moses Pillager, though for other reasons.

'Not everyone can see him. You might look right through him, like a ghost.'

'I have sharp eyes.'

'He doesn't speak.'

'I'll talk Indian.'

'That's not what I mean,' my uncle sighed.

I wouldn't quit. 'Why shouldn't I visit my cousin?'

'Moses isn't his real name,' Nanapush said at last. Rushes Bear left abruptly and then my uncle continued, but not with pleasure.

'When that first sickness came and thinned us out, Moses Pillager was still a nursing boy, the favourite of his mother, *Nanakawepenesick*, Different Thumbs, a woman who always had quick ideas. She didn't want to lose her son, so she decided to fool the spirits by pretending that Moses was already dead, a ghost. She sang his death song, made his gravehouse, laid spirit food upon the ground, put his clothes upon him backwards. His people spoke past him. He lived invisible, and he survived.

'And yet, though the sickness spared Moses, the cure bent his mind. He was never the same boy and later, when the coughing sickness swept through, he left us all for good and went to the island in Matchimanito, taking some cats he had stolen from the yard of an old Frenchwoman. The next winter he walked across the lake and appeared in town. His clothes were patched with the tanned and striped skins of cats. He walked with a cat's care, only backwards."

'I'm going over there,' I told Nanapush the next morning.

***

In the first extract, the adolescent boy, Marcus, a gifted pianist, is desperate to defend his piano teacher Madame Sousatzka from his dissatisfied mother, Mrs Crominski. The speech of these two characters differs in several ways. Marcus speaks standard English; his mother speaks as a foreigner (as in the inverted syntax of 'Nine months it is' and 'A beard you'll grow'). Marcus speaks in a reactive and defensive way ("'No!' Marcus shouted." And: "'She's the best teacher in London, Momma,' he begged."). The reader knows she is not the best teacher in London. Marcus exaggerates in desperation.

Even though Mrs Crominski acknowledges Madame Sousatzka is giving Marcus free lessons, she is sure enough of herself to insist that Marcus is wasting time with this teacher. The mother wants her son to give public recitals right now. The son, half in love with his piano teacher though not able to name this to himself, only wants to continue seeing her. The emotional tone of the characters' speech reflects their relative power. And, at this point, the mother still controls the son.

In the second extract the narrator, an older adolescent girl, a virgin, has decided to offer herself to a handsome, strange cousin. The parent figure, her uncle Nanapush, understanding her intentions, though she's only asked for information about her cousin Moses, counsels against the liaison. He speaks quietly, as opposed to Marcus's mother, and here the characters speak the same standard (North American) English. The dialogue proceeds at a much lower overtly emotional tone than in the first extract. The exception is the interjection by Rushes Bear, Nanapush's girlfriend, but having had her outburst, she leaves the scene, since she has no official status with the girl.

The dialogues also differ in larger contexts. The boy and his mother are culturally different. She remains essentially Eastern European. Marcus is culturally English and is beginning to struggle against his mother's single-parent domination. The cultural context of the second extract is more uniform. These are Ojibwe Indians living on a North Dakota reservation. Nevertheless, the girl's dialogue reveals that she won't be stopped by traditional beliefs:

'Not everybody can see him. You might look right through him like a ghost.'

'I have sharp eyes.'

'He doesn't speak.'

'I'll talk Indian.'

***

In both extracts, the parent figure gives a long speech. Mrs Crominski's is a tragicomic lament about the piano teacher's negative influence on Marcus.

'So all your life you'll stay with Madame Sousatzka. A beard you'll grow there and still you're not ready. [...] Have you ever heard such a thing! A boy should go for piano lessons and a hump he gets.'

Nanapush tells the tale of Moses Pillager (narration as dialogue). This is tragic and magic, a tale of death and of tricking death and of the price paid for tricking death.

Marcus gives way to his mother's lament and threat. The girl in *Love Medicine* calmly hears her uncle out (and later has erotic fantasies about Moses) and returns to Nanapush next morning to tell him – to tell, not ask – that she's going to Moses.

These extracts illustrate how the social-cultural context, every bit as much as the direct subject material of conflict, can determine the tone of the dialogue.

Another useful idea you can draw from these extracts involves the dramatic power of dialogue. On the surface, the extract from *Madame Sousatzka* has the more dramatic dialogue. His mother tells Marcus he should leave his piano teacher. The boy shouts back that he won't. He speaks of Madame Sousatzka in superlatives: 'I never understood the piano before I went to her.' And: 'She's the best piano teacher in London.' His mother's response is hyperbole: 'So many pieces. So much practising. What for, I'm asking. A beard you'll grow there and still you're not ready.' The exchange ends with a threat. The piano teacher has exactly one week to announce a date for Marcus's concert or she'll cease to be his teacher. Marcus speaks 'defiantly'. His mother is 'exasperated'.

In contrast, the extract from *Love Medicine* has only one dramatically expressed utterance, but that's spoken by Rushes Bear, and neither the girl nor her uncle responds to her. The dialogue between niece and uncle has no outbursts like that between son and mother. Its surface is calm. When the girl asks Nanapush to tell her about Moses, his first response is silence: 'He studied my face, his head to one side...'

And the uncle's objections, when he does speak, do not come across as dire warnings: 'You might look through him like a ghost.' And: 'He doesn't speak.' The girl's common-sense replies, like answers to a test, make these objections seem trivial. The emotions Nanapush does show are not, like Mrs Crominski's, highly dramatic: 'My uncle sighed.' And: '...my uncle continued, but not with pleasure.' These emotional highs are very low key.

Given these obvious differences between the extracts, it might be expected that the first extract would walk off with the dramatic prize. But that's not the case.

What charges the *Love Medicine* extract with dramatic power is the story that Nanapush tells the girl. He tells it calmly, without raising his voice, without gesticulation or exasperation. It is the details in this story about the lengths a mother will go to protect her child from death by making him behave as if he was not there, as if he were dead, that are so powerful. The lasting effect of this love, this cure, 'bent his mind'. You don't have to be of the speaker's culture to believe it. In fact, it is the quiet telling of this story that helps make it so powerful, even shocking. Nanapush tells it in a matter-of-fact way. It makes us understand the ironic power of a 'matter of fact', given these details. Moses Pillager has been made strange, perhaps mentally ill.

Mrs Crominski's long speech on the other hand, begins with 'So all your life...'. It is a verbal fantasy, a highly excited way of trying to convince Marcus through spur-of-the-moment exaggeration.

Dialogue can have great dramatic power without shouts, curses or threats, though there's nothing wrong with using them when they fit. This isn't to say that the second extract is better or worse writing than the first; it is to say – to offer an example of– how different characters can speak with each other to create the dramatic tension which reveals their character – who they are. Both extracts present believable, interesting, revealing dialogues which you can see, even in short extracts, move the story forward.

Write

Write a two-person dialogue of no more than two to three pages in which one character tries to explain/convince/warn/attract the other by telling a short anecdote or story of about 500–600 words. Remember that this anecdote/story has to be true to the cultural and interpersonal context of the characters.

How does a writer make different characters' voices sound different?

Listen to each of the following 11 statements as you read:

I am not going to do that.

I'm not doing that.

I won't do it.

I don't do things like that.

No, I don't think I can do that.

I wouldn't dream of doing that.

In your dreams.

No.

Never.

Are you serious?

You cannot be serious.

Here is a possible range of voices all communicating a negative response, all using a very basic vocabulary. Except for response 7, there are no colloquialisms, regional expressions or accents. While a single character might use all of them in different contexts and moods, it's also possible to make one or two of these – numbers 8 and 9, for example – the typical negative response of a taciturn or surly character. Responses 4 and 5 might be those of a quiet-spoken, self-assured character, and response 11 could be that of a sarcastic tennis player.

Key idea
Only a small variation in speech can create real distinction between characters' voices.

How can a writer actually hear his or her character's speech?

Key idea
The best way to hear your character's speech is to read it out loud.

When you read to yourself, you engage in sub-vocalization, a way of silently moving your vocal cords to inwardly sound the words. This is done so quickly and regularly that you're not really aware of it. Even if you became more aware of this, it's not what's meant in the Key idea above. Nor does 'read out loud' mean to whisper. Nor does 'read out loud' mean to say it at your reading speed, which is from two to ten times as fast as people speak. It means reading the words your character speaks (the speech, not the supporting narrative) at the same volume and pace as you intend your character to speak them. Embarrassing?

Get over it.

Close the door. Wait until everyone else is asleep. Go out to the backyard or garden or park or to the woods, if need be. But read it out loud. LISTEN to it as you read it out loud.

Are there writers who write great dialogue without having to do this? Doubtless there are. So what? You have to start training your ear for dialogue somewhere, and the beginning seems a logical place. Perhaps with practice and more practice your ear will be trained to hear your characters speak pretty much as you write it.

Just as your own speech is the primary source of the dialogue you write, your own ear is the primary source for testing that dialogue. If you have other sources, resources, such as a friend or family member, use them. Have them read your dialogue or read it aloud to them. (It's best if such people are not going to say that everything you write is perfect nor that everything you write is junk.)

Write

Make a list of ten or so statements or responses which essentially give the same information – positive or negative or neutral – but which use slightly different ordinary words. Next, read each of them out loud, listening. Then read them out loud again, listening. Then make any changes that occur to you and interest you in any of the statements. Finally, play around with your list by adding one or two less ordinary words. These words can be formal or informal or colloquial, etc.

Why play around?

Because you're a writer. Because you want to become a better writer. Asking you to play around, as above, can begin to show you how the slight variation of vocabulary can add strongly distinguishing qualities to a character's dialogue.

I have a friend who was raised in North Carolina as a child. He's lived the rest of his life away from there and not particularly among people with US southern accents. His voice is a standard, East Coast educated English with no regional accent. But when he's tense, one word changes in his speech. Rather than say 'I can't manage,' he says 'I *cain't* manage,' reverting to the way he pronounced it as a child. When I asked him about this, he said he thought it was part unconscious and part conscious, a way of personal emphasis. It just felt right for him.

Speak the following sentence out loud: 'It ain't necessarily so.'

You'll probably recognize it as a famous song title (by Ira Gershwin for his brother George Gershwin's opera *Porgy and Bess*). As a statement, it's a curious mix of vocabularies. Look at the following sentence groups:

A1   It isn't so.
A2   It isn't necessarily so.
B1   It ain't so.
B2   It ain't necessarily so.

A1 is a statement in standard English in which 'so' is the equivalent of 'like that'. Statement A2, also standard English, adds the qualifier 'necessarily'. This adverb is neither exotic nor arcane. B1 is a statement in colloquial English. It's straightforward and not particularly memorable. Statement B2, however, is more memorable, because it mixes the colloquial 'ain't' with the standard 'necessarily'. While the adverb is still the same word it was in statement A2, the reader/listener is now more aware of the length of this five-syllable word because of the shift of level of diction. And it's this that gives character and memorableness to the statement. Of course, this assumes it hasn't become clichéd through overuse since the 1930s.

At extreme levels of diction, the vocabulary of speech is entirely vulgarism and colloquialism or entirely formal, grammatical and learned. Most people's speaking vocabulary falls somewhere in between the extremes. It's a mix of formal and colloquial levels of English; people naturally vary the level of their speech according to audience and context. You speak to a four-year-old at one level of diction, to a friend at the pub at another, and as a witness in a trial at yet a third. Moreover, the level of language spoken is itself no guarantor of verbal coherence or expressive power. What works for the characters in Henry James' *The Golden Bowl* will not do for those in Hubert Selby's *Last Exit to Brooklyn*.

In characterization the rough-speaking rancher may have more clarity and eloquence in ordinary conversation than the professor of astrophysics; the opposite can just as likely be the case.

Focus point

Be wary of stereotyped language: it's often not the way people speak.

Write

Write a two-page dialogue between a country person (farmer, rancher, gardener, small shopkeeper, etc.) and a city professional (teacher, salesperson, accountant, doctor, stockbroker, etc.). They meet at a country pub or teashop or small restaurant.

Write it first so that it's clear from their levels of diction what their backgrounds are. Then revise it, making the diction of each more mixed, less stereotyped, to make it more vivid and interesting.

As stressed earlier, small variations in levels of speech, particular combinations of everyday words, can produce effectively differentiated voices between characters. However, the writer has many other variations, large and small, with which to create different voices for different characters, as illustrated in the following extracts:

Case study: Different voices

1

...the old professor was half asleep and as always when he was drowsy his lecture grew more and more unintelligible... 'And may we not say,' old Turner asked querulously, 'or perhaps it is too serious a thing to say – though Burke – or it may be Newman – I have forgotten which – remarks (though he qualifies the remark – and let me add in passing that whatever we may think – and think we must – though of course within certain limits...).'

2

He spoke quickly and clearly but with the accent of a half educated man... At last he left her, sniggering, 'to dispose of de dispatches as she tought best'.

3

Helen was almost giving up in despair when the man of the house, a tall, bony, good-natured lad, drove up the boreen in a country cart. 'The boys,' he said, 'were wesht beyont the hill in Crowley's, where all the boys wint, and likely they wouldn't be back before midnight. There was only Mike Redmond and Tom Jordan in it; the resht of the column got shcattered during the day.'

4

[Helen] remembered a habit of hers that had become a college joke, the habit of pulling younger girls aside and asking if there wasn't something wrong with her lip. Not that there ever was, but it provided the Darling with an excuse to pull a long face, and say with a sigh, 'Harry bit me, dear. Whatever am I going to do with that boy?'

5

'...And after ten minutes Tommy gave in and said with his best Sunday morning smile, "So sorry I must go, Commandant," and they solemnly shook hands again – just as though they wouldn't have liked to cut one another's throats instead!'

'But do you mean to say –?' Helen was incredulous. 'Do you really mean to say you don't bang the door in these people's faces?'

'Who do you mean?' asked the Darling with equal consternation. 'Is it Tommy Keogh and Vincent Kelly?'

'No, no. But Free State soldiers?'

'God, no!'

'You don't?'

'Not at all. I've known Vincent Kelly since he was that high. Why the devil *should* I bang the door in his face? I remember when he and Tommy were thick as thieves, when Vincent wouldn't go to a dance unless Tommy went too. Tomorrow they'll be as thick again – unless they shoot one another in the meantime... And you think I'm going to quarrel with one about the other?'

'Certainly not,' said Michael Redmond with dignity. 'No one expects impossibilities.'

'Of course not!' echoed Jordan, his voice tinged with the same elaborate irony.

Obviously he was enjoying Helen's discomfiture.

This range of speech and techniques for establishing different voices occur in one short story, 'Soirée Chez une Belle Jeune Fille', by Frank O'Connor. In most of the extracts, the narrative tells you the intended characterization in the voice.

In Extract 1, the sleepy old professor's words grow 'more and more unintelligible'. Old Turner begins to say 'And may we not say', but never gets around to saying what that is. Instead, another thought intrudes, and that thought is in turn unfinished as yet another thought breaks in, and the original thought recedes further and further from his memory and the listeners'/readers'. Turner is essentially talking in his sleep, talking nonsense, a nonsense of incoherent scholarly snippets. The extract is a little satire on learned meaninglessness.

Extract 2 presents 'the accent of a half educated man'. 'Dispose' and 'dispatches' show the education; 'de' (for 'the') and 'tought' (for 'thought') show the lack of education. And 'as she tought best' shows a combination of educated phrasing and uneducated pronunciation. The context of 'educated' and 'uneducated' is how it sounds to Helen, the story's protagonist, as she runs a message for the Irish Republican Army during the Irish Civil War of the early 1920s, when the IRA fought the newly formed Free State soldiers.

With Helen, we hear in Extract 3 the particular accent of a country 'lad'. The region is probably rural County Cork. Note that this isn't a lisp or other speech defect. He says 'wesht' for 'west', 'resht' for 'rest', and 'shcattered' for 'scattered'; but other 's' sounds – 'boys,' 'Crowley's' – have a standard pronunciation. He also says 'beyont' for 'beyond,' and 'wint' for 'went.' O'Connor, coming from Cork, would certainly know the accent, but this is perhaps coming close to a potential over-elaboration that could leave the general reader unsure of what is supposed to be heard.

Extract 4 develops through narrative to give the Darling's (her nickname) voice the background so that, when she finally speaks, we understand she's crazy about men. This establishes the tension between her and Helen in the final extract. Helen is a passionate partisan of the IRA men, Redmond and Jordan, in the room. The Darling's story shocks Helen in being so apolitical. The men, used to the Darling, seem to take her story in their stride, further bewildering Helen. This seemingly light-hearted scene soon turns very dark.

O'Connor has had to develop the character contrast carefully between the two women to enable us to fully 'hear' rather than just to read the dialogue in this scene.

How can the writer avoid dialogue stereotypes in age and gender?

As with general dialogue, the source of writing the dialogue of children and of old people is you. Since we've all been children, memory is important. If you have children, your observation and your ear have models and teachers to hand. And family can offer the examples of speech in old age. If this isn't the case, just listen. There are children and old people around you. In conceiving of their dialogue in your fiction, a good starting attitude is that children are people. Old people are people. Children may have less experience and less factual knowledge than adults, but this doesn't make them stupid. The old may move slowly and be hard of hearing, but they have experience and intelligence, and if their short-term memory isn't as good as it used to be, their longer memories can be splendidly detailed. They may not speak the slang you do, but neither do you speak the slang a 12-year-old uses. This means you have to use your ears and your imagination, as usual, to get it right.

Today, getting it right with children's talk may involve directly questioning a child you know. The child of ten or eleven is much more likely to use diction influenced by the technology of mobile phones, text mail and computer games. Nothing ages faster than children's colloquialisms and slang, and IT is constantly speeding this up. As with adult jargon, knowing your child characters' interests (music, sports, comics, etc.) can give you a key to their language. As in adult speech, children often mix levels of diction; they are, as we were, trying out new words they've come across. At times, they may not fully understand particular words they use.

In J.D. Salinger's short story 'For Esmé, With Love and Squalor', the traumatized narrator, a writer serving in World War II, is asked by Esmé to write her a story with 'squalor', having come across and being fascinated by the word though not fully understanding its depths. She's a bright and lonely 13-year-old whose dialogue is believable, memorable and touching. This is achieved by having Esmé, a war orphan, speak with no self-pity and use a precocious vocabulary some of which she doesn't understand, in an effort not to be 'childish and silly'. Asking the narrator to write a story, she says she wants it:

> '...exclusively for me sometime. I'm an avid reader.'
>
> I told her I certainly would if I could. I said that I wasn't terribly prolific.
>
> 'It doesn't have to be terribly prolific. Just so that it isn't childish and silly.' She reflected.
>
> 'I prefer stories about squalor.'
>
> 'About what?' I said, leaning forward. 'Squalor. I'm extremely interested in squalor.'

This combination of unexpected sophistication undercut by pretensions of understanding ('It doesn't have to be terribly prolific') make her amusing and interesting.

Note Salinger's techniques. For emphasizing Esmé's speech, he puts the narrator's speech into indirect quotation ('I told her...'). And to speed up the moment of the narrator's confusion, Salinger breaks from his general convention of a separate paragraph to mark a change of speaker ('...I said, leaning forward. "Squalor. I'm extremely interested in squalor."').

Salinger went on to create one of the most convincing voices of conflicted adolescence in his character Holden Caulfield, the 16-year-old narrator of *The Catcher in the Rye*. A bit of the 1940s–1950s slang might be dated, but this voice grabs the reader from the novel's opening sentence. Though literally narration, it is exactly the voice of Caulfield's dialogue.

> If you really want to hear about it, the first thing you'll probably want to know is where I was born, and what my lousy childhood was like, and how my parents were occupied and all before they had me, and all that David Copperfield kind of crap, but I don't feel like going into it.

It is the rhythm, the spilling over of the sound ('is where...' 'and what...' 'and how...'); the repetition ('and all before...' 'and all that...'); the barely suppressed anger ('really', 'lousy', and 'crap'); the showing off of culture and rejection of it at the same time in the conjunction of 'David Copperfield' with 'crap'; and the overall refusal to do what is wanted ('If you really want to know...') with the explanation that is no explanation – 'I don't feel like going into it.' It is this perfect ear for speech that grabs you by sounding so authentic.

Are there gender distinctions in dialogue? No and yes. An example of no could be Marcus in *Madame Sousatzka*. You could imagine him to be a talented young girl pianist and have pretty much the same dialogue. And the narrator of *Love Medicine* in this chapter's first Case study could likewise be male. (But I don't know if this would be accurate in the cultural context of the Ojibwe Indians at the time and place of the setting.) And yes, there are distinctions. It's difficult to hear the Caulfield voice above as a girl's, though this isn't because of its aggression. It may have to do with the combination of aggression and the showing off of the Copperfield reference that I find more typifies male than female behaviour in the same social and period contexts. Esmé's voice seems more a girl's than a boy's at that age because of its politeness and direct appeal to the narrator she's just met to have him write her a story. Not in the extract is the fact that she's left her adult companion in a teashop and come over to the narrator's table to initiate a conversation. Given the conventions of class and date of the setting, this would be very unlikely behaviour from a 13-year-old boy. Unlikely, mind you, but not impossible.

For what it's worth, in my teaching and reading experience, I find more male writers have problems with female voices than the other way around. But there are women writers who have trouble with male voices and characters as well as men writers who create believable female voices and characters. To be honest, I have difficulty creating believable women in my fiction. But I am aware of it and have the great good luck of having a woman partner who is a good writer and will tell me, as she reads or listens to a draft of mine, that a woman would never say that or do that, or words to that effect. So back I go to get it as right as I can.

You should do the same. First, in showing/reading your writing draft to people of the other gender, see if their feedback, unprompted, finds a problem with the voice and character as a function of gender. Second, if not, prompt them; ask if the female/male character(s) are convincing, seem authentic in gender.

The best, the only, way to work out any gender problem of dialogue (and of narrative action) is to work it out by rewriting, by considering who this person really is in the context of your entire piece of fiction and in the particular scene. If you do have a problem with gender, you will, with practice, be able to write that man or woman better.

 Focus point

Many problems with gender can be solved if you think of your character first as a person, not first as a male or a female.

 Write

Go to a scene of dialogue in a short story or novel you admire and set down the elements of dialogue that differentiate the female and male characters. Are they really elements of gender rather than of non-gendered points of view? What elements of context are involved? Make sure you write this out rather than just think of it, so that you make your thoughts on this visible and memorable to yourself.

 Focus points

Chapter 2 began to look in some detail at how a writer can build a character's voice. The chapter's main ideas are summarized in the following five points:

- Characters come to life not only by what they say but also by how they say it, by what they sound like. Although you write dialogue from extending your own speech, the speech of others, and speech heard and read in other modes, not all writers find that creating convincing dialogue comes easily, especially at the beginning of their writing careers. Making character notes can help this process. Typically, you'll want to set down your character's name, age, physical appearance and occupation as well as various aspects of background such as parentage, place(s) raised and education. One or other of these might lead to listing some aspects of character or emotional temperament, or listing leisure interests or type of reading your character chooses. You should remember to keep from setting down the character's voice or manner of speaking until you have a good number of other character notes.

- Character reveals itself in dialogue when there's some level of tension or conflict. This often takes the form of one character trying to convince another to take or not to take a particular course of action. Such dialogue can incorporate longer speeches as anecdote or story meant to convince; these can add variety to the shorter to-and-fro statements between the characters.

- Quite small variations in speech can create real differences between characters' voices. These variations need not involve different vocabularies, levels of diction or accents.

- To write good dialogue, you need to develop your ability to really hear the speech you write for your characters. The best way to learn to do this is to read that dialogue out loud. This forces you to read it at a speaking pace, rather than at the much faster reading pace. Overcome your shyness. Read it to a friend, partner, or fellow writer to get feedback on whether it sounds convincing.

- Avoid writing stereotyped dialogue for children and the other gender by first thinking of the child or of the woman or of the man as a person. When writing a young person's slang or colloquial speech in a contemporary setting, check it out if possible with a young person. If this isn't possible, listen carefully when you're out: their slang and jargon changes (dates) quickly. Do the same in checking for any unconvincing speech from a female/male character by reading your dialogue or having it read by someone of the same gender as that character.

Chapter 3 is about narrative in dialogue. Do you need it? What do you need it for? How much of it is right? The chapter uses a range of examples to show you how writers have answered these questions.

3

Narrative in dialogue

In this chapter you will learn:
- When to use 'identifying narrative' – i.e. stating who is speaking
- About using descriptive narrative in dialogue
- About other forms of narrative that are useful in writing dialogue
- How to avoid overuse of the single adverb as descriptive narrative.

Here's a scene of dialogue from the first part of a short story. There has been an ice storm.

'Can the trains go in this weather? I don't see how they can do.'

'I talked to him on the phone yesterday. He's coming.'

'How did he sound?' my mother said.

To my annoyance, she began to hum to herself.

I said, 'He's had rotten news about his work. Terrible, in fact.'

'Explain his work to me again,' she said.

'He's a plant taxonomist.'

'Yes?' my mother said. 'What does that mean?'

'It means he doesn't have a lot of money,' I said. 'He studies grasses. He said on the phone he's been turned down for a research grant that would have meant a great deal to us. Apparently the work he's been doing for the past seven or so years is irrelevant or outmoded. I guess "superficial" is what he told me.'

'I won't mention it to him, then.' My mother said.

'Pretty Ice', by Mary Robison

There are two sorts of narrative in this extract: identifying narrative ('my mother said', 'she said', 'I said') and what could be called descriptive/informative narrative. This latter kind occurs only once, above, as 'To my annoyance, she began to hum to herself.' The mother is driving her daughter, the narrator, to pick up her daughter's fiancé from the train station. The narrator and her fiancé haven't seen each other for over a year, and the mother has never met him. The reader at this point understands that the narrator is naturally anxious, and that her 'annoyance' comes from her mother's seeming lack of interest in the answer to her own question by humming.

The narrative statement seems to be building the nervous tension in the daughter about meeting her fiancé after so long an absence. It also shows an irritation with her mother. But what exactly is the point of this irritation? Given that there is a considerable amount of tension/ conflict already – the imminint meeting after long separation, the difficult, even potentially dangerous, weather, why add a third strand? If we know the entire story (sorry to have to give the plot away), we see that only a few minutes after picking up her fiancé from the station, the narrator understands she wants nothing further to do with him: he demonstrates that he has nothing in common with her deeper values.

The annoyance referred to is only one of three. At the start of the story, the narrator is annoyed at her mother honking the car horn when she picks her up, and after the extract, she's annoyed that her mother hasn't taken the most direct route to the train station. But at the climax, when the mother stops the car to look at a beautifully ice-bound tree and the fiancé's response is only to explain the harm the ice will do to the tree's fibres, the narrator knows that, despite her annoyance with her mother, she is, at heart, so much more like her mother than like this unfeeling 'superficial' man in the back seat.

This is an example of how the placement of small bits of descriptive/ informative narration within a scene of dialogue can subtly develop meaning and feeling in the story. The narrator understands that her annoyance with her mother is 'superficial'; that her identification with her mother's values is deep.

Key idea

Even small bits of narrative can greatly develop plot and theme when well placed in scenes of dialogue. In retrospect, they reveal more than they seem to at the time of first reading.

Does a writer need identifying narrative?

No, not very much of it, especially in a two-person dialogue.

...I guess I'd have to say that would be an oyster.

A mountain oyster or a real oyster?

A real oyster.

How were they cooked?

They weren't cooked. They just laid there in their shells. You put hotsauce on them.

You ate that?

I did.

How'd it taste?

About like you'd expect.

Cormac McCarthy, *All the Pretty Horses*

There's no need for identifying narrative here. However, the extract is immediately preceded with 'Strangest thing I ever ate, said Blevins. I guess...' What McCarthy wants here, and throughout his writing, is the least amount of identifying narrative consistent with clarity. He wants the reader to hear the conversation as it actually occurs, without narrative interruption as much as possible. Immediately after the extract, when a new, third, character joins the conversation, McCarthy identifies him:

> About like you'd expect.
>
> They sat watching the fire.
>
> Where you from, Blevins? said Rawlins.

Note that while McCarthy does not use quotation marks for dialogue, he does use the convention of a new paragraph for each change of speaker. Some writers use a dash at the start of each paragraph of dialogue in place of quotation marks. Most writers use quotation marks and new paragraphs for change of speaker.

 ## Write

Write at least a half-page of dialogue between two characters without using identifying narrative. Make most of the statements of each character relatively short, no more than one or two sentences. Avoid references to each other by name or by age or gender or any other way that would clearly identify them. The idea is to have the reader 'overhear' two people speaking.

How does descriptive/ informative narrative appear in dialogue?

In its shortest form, descriptive/informative narrative is appended to the identifying narrative to become part of the dialogue statement:

> 'I never could,' Amy said mournfully.

The addition of the adverb 'mournfully' to the identifying 'Amy said' describes how Amy said the words 'I never could'. It tells the reader with what sort of emotional tone the words were spoken. This could work well in a particular context.

However, from the second half of the twentieth century and continuing, you find that many writers and teachers of literature and of writing warn you away from using this brief bit of descriptive narrative to qualify how the dialogue was said. The primary reason for this is that such adverbs are no substitute for emotional tone within the actual dialogue. And the examples that writers and teachers point to are found in badly written books in which the dialogue is clichéd because the characters are mere stereotypes. Such writing tries to make up for the absolute blandness of its dialogue by adding such adverbs as if they were the spice to give the speeches some flavour. They don't. They show the speeches up for the flat and predictable and purely generic, as opposed to individualistic, talk they are. What's more, the adverbs from such writers tend themselves to be clichés. They are of the nature of:

'Then I will *make* you mine,' he said masterfully.

'Hi,' the little girl said winningly.

This doesn't mean that you should never use the one-word adverb as descriptive narrative; it means you should use it with care. Good writers do use it, but you find they often put the one-word descriptive narrative into more descriptive verbs than 'said'. Back in Chapter 1, you read Richard Russo writing, '"Put on a clean shirt before you go out front," Miles reminded him.' Here, 'reminded' tells you much more about Miles and his relationship with his slightly reprobate father than 'said' would have. And from Chapter 2, in the extract from *Love Medicine*, Louise Erdrich writes: '"That's not what I mean," my uncle sighed.' Again, the verb is used as descriptive narrative in a more specific way than 'said'.

In the same Case study, Bernice Rubens wrote: '"For me, you're ready, Marcus," she said solemnly…' Here the adverb works. It's justified because it marks a change in tone from the usual high-pitched, excited stream of words from Mrs Crominski.

 ## Write

Pick up a book you think badly written and find and write out five examples of single adverbs that don't really add anything as descriptive narrative. By each, write a few words explaining why it doesn't work. Then pick up a book you think well written and write out five examples of single-word descriptive narrative – adverbs and verbs – that do work. By each write a few words explaining why.

Focus point

Take care using single adverbs as descriptive narrative. They can be effective, but they cannot substitute for emotional tone missing in the actual dialogue.

What other shorter forms of narrative are useful in writing dialogue?

Writers interject separate clauses and single sentences into dialogue. This is often a good technique when you sense you're depending too much on single adverbs that aren't specific enough or that sound hackneyed. In another Case study from Chapter 2, you read: '...and said with his best Sunday morning smile...'. This is very different than 'and said smilingly'.

'Smilingly' can mean any sort of smile. What O'Connor has added is a smile of purity, a smile of sincerity, and a smile of grace; and yet by qualifying it with 'his best' there is a suggestion that he has a range of Sunday morning smiles and that this may be put on and insincere. In the deeply ironic context of the scene being described, the smile has an additional ambiguity in being related by a narrator whose neutrality is held in contempt by the other main characters.

William Trevor's short story 'Men of Ireland' tells of a street person, Donal Prunty, a beggar and petty thief, who returns to the Ireland he fled in disgrace years earlier to extort money from his old village priest, Father Meade. He does this by insinuation and outright lying that, as an altar boy, he was sexually abused by Meade. Meade, though innocent, fears scandal and gives Prunty all the cash in the house.

This first extract is from the early part of the story.

Case study: William Trevor, 'Men of Ireland'

'Would you remember me, Father? Would you remember Donal Prunty?'

Miss Brehany came in with the water and observed Father Meade's slow nod, after a pause.

She was thanked for the glass of water.

'Are you Donal Prunty?' Father Meade asked.

'I served at the Mass for you, Father.'

'It wasn't yourself who buried my mother.'

'Father Laughlin if it wasn't myself. You went away, Donal.'

'I did all right. I was never back till now.'

He was begging. Father Meade knew, you always could, it was one of the senses that developed in a priest. Not that a lot came begging in a scattered parish, not like you'd get in the town.

The first narrative paragraph in this extract appears as the follow-up to Father Meade's earlier request for water when his housekeeper, Miss Brehany, wakes the old priest from napping to tell him there's a visitor. But it contributes much more than the realistic business of the household. Meade's 'slow' nod reminds the reader of his age and his drowsiness, as does his 'pause'. The paragraph's second sentence shows the writer's great skill at showing, while telling. 'She was thanked' would communicate the literal meaning of the nod. The reader already knows that it's the water he's thanking her for, but Trevor writes it all out. In reading 'She was thanked for the glass of water,' you hear the slow, deliberate pace of the old priest. You sense the set habits of his daily life which Prunty's sudden appearance disturbs. This helps to make us believe, later on, in the priest's confusion. Habit is still strong in him, memory is weaker.

The second narrative paragraph, with its blunt opening, 'He was begging', shows Father Meade is no fool. Note the shift from third person ('Father Meade knew') to second person ('you always could') in the second sentence. This shifts us closer to the priest's own voice, and the final sentence – 'Not that a lot came begging in a scattered parish, not like you'd get in the town' – is the priest's own internal voice. Narrative can be very flexible, mediating between the omniscient third-person viewpoint and the first-person voice, making itself appear a more natural part of the scene of dialogue. Of course, this isn't natural; it's the writer's art.

The next extract follows from the first as they walk in the large, pleasant garden of the church house.

***

Father Meade unlatched the French doors and went ahead of his visitor. 'I'm fond of the garden,' he said, not turning his head.
'I'm on the streets, Father.'
'In Dublin, is it?'
'I went over to England, Father.'
'I think I maybe heard.'
'What work was there here, all the same?'
'Oh, I know. I know. Nineteen... what would it have been?'
'Nineteen eighty-one I went across.'
'You had no luck there?'
'I never had luck, Father.

The old man walked slowly, the arthritis he was afflicted with in the small bones of both his feet a nuisance today.

[They walk in the garden and the reader learns in narration the set-up of this parish property. Then the narration goes into the priest's reflections on the garden. He's thinking about the Virginia creeper turning red when the following thought comes to him.]

Prunty had got into trouble. The recollection was vague at first, before more of it came back: something about stealing from farms at harvest time or the potato planting, when everyone would be in the fields. Always the same, except when he was caught with the cancer charity box. As soon as his mother was buried he went off and was in trouble again before he left the district a year or so later.

***

It is the garden, the priest's stated fondness for it, that gets Prunty's reaction, 'I'm on the streets, Father.' The writer uses the narrative of setting to further character in dialogue: to Prunty, the idea of pleasure taken by being outdoors is an affront. The garden goes with the house, the priest has both, so it's easy for him to talk about the pleasure of it. The self-pity is made tangible by this combination of narrative setting and dialogue response.

The next narrative in this dialogue comes just after another of Prunty's self-pitying statements: 'I never had luck, Father.' The narrative literally communicates information about Father Meade's arthritis. Its expression as 'a nuisance today' metaphorically extends to what Prunty is to the priest. Also of significance is that the priest does not complain of his affliction.

Finally, as they walk, Father Meade begins to recollect things Prunty has done. That he cares nothing for the local society of which he's a part is indicated by his stealing when he knows everyone will be away from their homes working. As if this weren't bad enough, he steals a charity box, likely to have been in the church, and not just any charity but a cancer charity. Can there be anything worse than stealing from the poor and the sick? There is. What the reader knows from the very beginning of the story, and what Father Meade has forgotten or mixed up, is that Prunty has skipped town the day *before* his mother's funeral. Perhaps the priest is incapable of thinking Prunty so bad as to dishonour his mother. (The reader has earlier seen Prunty cynically lie about his mother in an attempt to cadge money from a driver who gives him a lift.) The narrative recollection of one character gains power here from what he does not know, gets wrong, but what the reader does know. This is a powerful device in fiction.

After some small talk about the changes in the village, Prunty asks Father Meade if he could give him some money. Though the priest acknowledges the request, on their way back to the room where they'd met, once inside, he offers Prunty a recommendation to a place in the village where he can find work. Prunty replies, 'It wasn't work I came for, Father.' The next extract directly follows this reply.

Prunty sat down. He took out a pack of cigarettes, and then stood up again to offer it to the priest. Father Meade was standing by the French doors. He came further into the room and stood behind his desk, not wanting to sit down himself because it might be taken as an encouragement by his visitor to prolong his stay. He waved the cigarettes away.

'I wouldn't want to say it,' Prunty said.

He was experiencing difficulty with his cigarette, failing to light it although he struck two matches, and Father Meade wondered if there was something the matter with his hands the way he couldn't keep them steady. But Prunty said the matches were damp. You spent a night sleeping out and you got damp all over even though it didn't rain on you.

'What is it you don't want to say, Mr. Prunty?'

Prunty laughed. His teeth were discoloured, almost black.

'Why're you calling me Mr. Prunty, Father?'

The priest managed a laugh, too. Put it down to age, he said; he sometimes forgot a name and then it would come back.

'Donal, it is,' Prunty said.

'Of course it is. What is it you want to say, Donal?'

'Things happened the time I was a server, Father.'

'It was a little later you went astray, Donal.'

'Have you a drink, Father? Would you offer me a drink?'

'We'll get Rose to bring us a cup of tea.'

Prunty shook his head, a slight motion, hardly a movement at all.

'I don't keep strong drink,' Father Meade said. 'I don't take it myself.'

'You used to give me a drink.'

'Ah no, no. What is it you want, Donal?'

'I'd estimate it was money, Father. [...]'

From here, Prunty's insinuations of being abused by Father Meade come thicker and faster as the story approaches its climax. And it's the two longer stretches of narrative at the start of this extract that begin the acceleration.

The first, beginning with 'Prunty sat down', is standard third-person narration. It describes what Prunty does. It goes on to describe not just what the priest does but what he thinks. The next narrative paragraph, beginning 'He was experiencing...', is more complex in point of view. The first sentence begins by describing what Prunty does, and then its second main clause shifts to Father Meade's thoughts. The next sentence shifts to Prunty in an indirect quote, and the final sentence continues the indirect quote without identifying narrative so that it comes even closer to representing Prunty's speech.

The effect of these slight, continuous shifts of viewpoint is, besides giving information, to add tension, a back-and-forth in form that mirrors the argument in the dialogue. Another tension this second paragraph of narrative adds is the suspense between Prunty's 'I wouldn't want to say it' – itself a mysterious blurting out of feeling – and the priest's question (and the reader's) 'What is it you don't want to say, Mr. Prunty?' And then, the question asked, the narrative once again holds off the answer in continuing with 'Prunty laughed. His teeth were discoloured, almost black.' The effect, whatever the sound of the laughter may have been, is unpleasant, since only Prunty's rotten teeth are observed/described.

This extract ends as Prunty says he's here asking for money. His insinuations grow stronger and cruder from this point. (It's worth pointing out that the final statement of the extract is the start of a longish paragraph of low-life lyricism from Prunty. Trevor, fine writer that he is, insists on the humanity of even a thoroughly immoral character like Prunty.)

The final extract occurs after Prunty accuses Father Meade of giving him wine to drink in the vestry when he was an altar boy, of telling him they were having a birthday party, of asking him to close his eyes. Prunty has also spoken of being joined in England by a woman named Eulala, who 'came over with a priest's infant inside her'. The priest keeps denying these accusations and asks Prunty not to say bad things. He even orders Prunty to leave, but Prunty stays, waiting for some money. Finally, the priest calls Prunty a liar.

'Tell your tale in Stacey's bar, Prunty, and maybe you'll be believed.'

Father Meade stood up and took what coins there were from his trouser pocket and made a handful of them on the desk.
'Make your confession, Prunty. Do that at least.'

Prunty stared at the money, counting it with his eyes. Then he scooped it up. 'If we had a few notes to go with it,' he said, 'we'd have the sum done right.'

He spoke slowly, as if unhurried enunciation was easier for the elderly. It was all the talk, he said, the big money there'd be. No way you could miss the talk, no way it wouldn't affect you.

He knew he'd get more. Whatever was in the house he'd go away with, and he watched while a drawer was unlocked and opened, while money was taken from a cardboard box. None was left behind.

'Thanks, Father,' he said before he went.

***

The first narrative paragraph here is third-person description of what the priest does. It appears to be a final take-it-and-get-out gesture. But Father Meade's dialogue is separated into a new paragraph. Why? Well, one thing this achieves is to isolate his contemptuous offer of loose change from the heartfelt plea for Prunty to do the right thing for the sake of his soul. Another is that it slows the pace at which the scene takes place. Prunty's paragraph, following, combines the descriptive narrative with the dialogue. When he scoops up the change, Prunty is in conman mode, and he immediately thinks to ask for bigger money.

The next paragraph, formally all narrative, describes Prunty having spoken slowly, as if to make it easier for the old priest to understand. But this is also a grotesque version of Father Meade's slow pace, the slowness not only of the old but a kind of mock attitude of caring for another person, which Prunty cannot do. The next sentence is indirect quotation only in not having quotation marks. The final sentence, shifting to second person, could also be direct speech but for the absence of the marks. The effect is to shift actual dialogue into a form of speaking half between the speaker Prunty and how the speech is heard by Father Meade, as if at a remove, as if he's hardly listening any more. What Prunty is actually saying in these last two sentences is that since everyone was talking about the open scandal in the Catholic Church in Ireland, you couldn't really blame a man for trying to cash in.

The penultimate paragraph in the extract is third-person narration limited to Prunty's thoughts and viewpoint. It's described with a dream-like inevitability. And why not, since it's as good as Prunty's wildest dreams of getting something, a good deal of something, for nothing. But what does this say of the priest? He doesn't protest, he says not a word but gives Prunty 'Whatever was in the house,' all of it. And, as in a dream, Father Meade's motives are mysterious. He wasn't guilty of anything, none of the other parish priests were guilty. Was it done just to have the peace of getting Prunty out of the house, the village, the country? Was it done because the priest felt, at some level, a responsibility to take on the sins of the clergymen who had done the 'sickening and terrible and disgraceful' things of Prunty's accusation? Or was the priest just old, tired and, finally, confused and frightened?

Two further points about this Case study. First, it was of necessity long and complex because of the variety of narrative effects and the necessity to discuss them in full context. There's no question that this is often difficult to work out. But studying the craft of writing isn't always a matter of 'a few simple tips and tricks' and Bob's your uncle.

Second, do not despair of achieving a complex range of narrative-dialogue effects. William Trevor did it through his talents, yes, but also through his long practice of writing.

Practice. Practice. And study good writing, too.

 ## Key idea

Narrative can be very flexible, moving between third-person omniscience towards near dialogue. This means it can help control the pace as well as the tone of scenes of dialogue.

 ## Write

Using a scene of dialogue you've written either for Write or as part of a piece of your own fiction, revise it by incorporating one of the more complex narrative techniques from the 'Men of Ireland' Case study above. It should be one that appeals to you and seems potentially useful to the development of character and/or the context of your dialogue and/or your plot. Don't worry about 'copying'. You're trying out a piece of advice or two on narrative technique. It will be your writing in your words.

WHAT ELSE CAN BE LEARNED ABOUT NARRATIVE FROM THIS CASE STUDY?

Earlier in this chapter, I discussed the potential problem of one-word descriptive narrative adverbs added to the identifying narration. Now look back over the Case study extracts from William Trevor's 'Men of Ireland' to see how many of these adverbs the extracts contain.

These extracts weren't chosen to look at the absence of these adverbs, but it is typical of much contemporary fiction. Having looked at some negative reasons – reasons to *avoid* any dependence on the single adverb for 'explaining' the speech – it's useful now to look at positive alternatives.

There are often more effective ways than the single adverb to characterize (to qualify) dialogue:

- use of a specific verb in place of 'said' or 'says'
- use of a dependent clause modifying the identifying narrative
- use of a separate sentence of descriptive/informative narrative
- use of a separate paragraph modifying preceding dialogue and/ or developing further ideas.

The extract from Mary Robison's 'Pretty Ice' at the beginning of this chapter has the following example:

'How did he sound?' my mother said.

To my annoyance, she began to hum to herself.

If this had been written

'How did he sound?' my mother said and began to hum to herself annoyingly.

the reader would have figured out that it was the narrator-daughter who was annoyed, but the annoyance would have been less part of the daughter's increasing tension than when stated in a separate sentence/paragraph in which she names 'my annoyance.'

In the second William Trevor extract, we find:

The old man walked slowly, the arthritis he was afflicted with in the small bones of both his feet felt a nuisance today.

If this were

The old man walked slowly, arthritically.

the shorter sentence would have been faster, and it is the slower sentence which better 'shows' the walk rather than tells it. In the same way, without 'the small bones of both his feet', the excruciating detail, the pain-creating detail, would be gone. What's more, the word 'nuisance' wouldn't be there and neither would its connection with Prunty. Prunty at this point is a nuisance. By the end of the dialogue, he has 'afflicted' Father Meade. All of this is in the subordinate clause modifying 'slowly'.

The third Trevor extract begins with: '"I wouldn't want to say it," Prunty said.' If it read '"I wouldn't want to say it," Prunty said mysteriously,' or '"I wouldn't want to say it," Prunty said hesitatingly,' or even 'Prunty said hesitatingly, mysteriously,' it would in no way substitute for the paragraph of narrative that follows. That paragraph shows the nervous hesitancy in the shaky hands (which also suggest alcoholism). It leads to Prunty's self-pitying rationalization that the matches were damp because he slept rough. Also gone would be the deliberation of Prunty's ad lib performance of appealing to the priest's pity while at the same time finding a way to work up the courage or anger to make his accusations of abuse. This narrative is vital to the deep characterization in the story – of both Prunty and Father Meade – which is dependent on pace.

 Focus point

Descriptive/informative narrative in scenes of dialogue develops the characterization and plot as well as the dialogue.

Do these narrative techniques exist only in more contemporary fiction?

No, they've been around for a long time, as in the following from the novel *Washington Square* by Henry James, written in 1881.

Case study: Henry James, *Washington Square*

The novel is a dark comedy of manners that tells the story of Catherine Slope, heiress of her cold domineering father, Dr Slope. There is no Mrs Slope. She died giving birth to Catherine. Her father strongly disapproves of Catherine's suitor, Morris Townsend, believing him to be attracted to Catherine because of her money. He has threatened to disinherit Catherine if she marries Townsend, and he's forbidden the suitor to visit his daughter. Slope's widowed sister, Lavinia Penniman, is set on helping Catherine's romance flourish. In this scene, she has just informed Catherine that she's met with Townsend.

...It seemed to her that her aunt was meddlesome; and from this came a vague apprehension that she would spoil something.

'I don't see why you should have seen him. I don't think it was right,' Catherine said.

'I was so sorry for him – it seemed to me some one ought to see him.'

'No one but I,' said Catherine, who felt as if she were making the most presumptuous speech of her life, and yet at the same time had an instinct that she was right in doing so.

'But you wouldn't, my dear,' Aunt Lavinia rejoined, 'and I didn't know what might become of him.'

'I have not seen him because my father has forbidden it,' Catherine said, very simply.

There was a simplicity in this, indeed, which fairly vexed Mrs. Penniman. 'If your father forbade you to go to sleep, I suppose you would keep awake!' she commented.

Catherine looked at her. 'I don't understand you. You seem to me very strange.'

'Well, my dear, you will understand me some day!'

Mrs. Penniman, who was reading the evening paper, which she perused daily from the first line to the last, resumed her occupation. She wrapped herself in silence; she was determined Catherine should ask her for an account of her interview with Morris. But Catherine was so silent for so long that she almost lost patience; and she was on the point of remarking to her that she was very heartless, when the girl at last spoke.

'What did he say?' she asked.

'He said he is ready to marry you any day, in spite of everything.'

Catherine made no answer to this, and Mrs. Penniman almost lost patience again; owing to which she at last volunteered the information that Morris looked very handsome, but terribly haggard.

'Did he seem sad?' asked her niece.

'He was dark under the eyes,' said Mrs. Penniman. 'So different from when I first saw him; though I am not sure that if I had seen him in this condition the first time, I should not have been even more struck with him. There is something brilliant in his very misery.'

This was, to Catherine's sense, a vivid picture, and though she disapproved, she felt herself gazing at it. 'Where did you see him?' she asked, presently.

'In – in the Bowery; at a confectioner's,' said Mrs. Penniman, who had a general idea that she ought to dissemble a little.

'Whereabouts is the place?' Catherine inquired, after another pause.

'Do you wish to go there, my dear?' said her aunt.

'Oh, no.' And Catherine got up from her seat and went to the fire, where she stood looking awhile at the glowing coals.

'Why are you so dry, Catherine?' Mrs. Penniman said at last.

'So dry?'

'So cold – so irresponsive?'

The girl turned very quickly. 'Did he say that?'

Mrs. Penniman hesitated a moment. 'I will tell you what he said. He said he feared only one thing – that you would be afraid.'

'Afraid of what?'

'Afraid of your father.'

Catherine turned back to the fire again, and then, after a pause, she said, 'I *am* afraid of my father.'

***

Is James depending too much on the adverb as narrative in '"I have not seen him because my father has forbidden it," Catherine said, very simply.'? Not at all. For one thing, she may say it very simply, but such absolute, unquestioning obedience, in spite of her genuine love for her suitor Morris, is not necessarily what might be taken for granted, especially not by the romantic Lavinia Penniman. For another, the adverb is used carefully; it's immediately picked up in the next line: 'There was a simplicity in this, indeed, which fairly vexed Mrs. Penniman.' Here the meaning has shifted from simple as pure and natural and direct, to simplicity which is akin to backwardness or stupidity, in the aunt's estimation.

Catherine is not sophisticated, but she is intelligent, more so than she's given credit for by her aunt. So James starts this dialogue scene with narrating Catherine's feeling about her aunt being 'meddlesome' and 'from this came a vague apprehension that she should spoil something'. Of course Catherine cannot know, because she has not experienced secret meetings or going behind her father's back, exactly what is wrong with her aunt meeting her suitor (behind her father's back). But it is this mood of 'vague apprehension', of something not quite right that exists through the dialogue that follows. It is like a stage direction to the writer to keep Catherine turning away, turning back, staring into the fire, turning back quickly. And this provides a heightening of the tension directly presented in the verbal confrontation between the two women.

The tension is also driven by the writer's use of silence between the characters. Who will speak first becomes more than a test of wills. It will be proof of how much Catherine cares, despite knowing that it is somehow wrong for her aunt to have such a clandestine meeting with her banned suitor. But Mrs Penniman doesn't quite get what the reader understands. She is angered by what she mistakes for her niece's coldness at not at all wanting to have her own secret rendezvous with Morris. But when she accuses Catherine of coldness, James writes: 'The girl turned very quickly. "Did he say that?"' She isn't interested in her aunt's feelings about her but in Morris's feelings. It is how she turns as well as what she asks that convinces us. This is the romantic climax of the scene, though the aunt's ego doesn't allow her to understand it. Catherine is deeply in love, for the first time in her life. She cannot yet conceive that she will have to disobey her beloved father to obey her love for Morris.

In all of this, James shows himself to be using narrative in ways that are contemporary, by enhancing the showing element. An interesting example of taking a very ordinary phrase, a near cliché, 'a vivid picture', and making something original of it, occurs after Catherine's aunt says, '"There is something brilliant in his very misery."' This is almost the quintessence of a certain romanticism which finds pale and haggard suffering for love, suffering with dark circles under its eyes, wildly, erotically attractive. Catherine senses this ('she disapproved') yet cannot resist: '…and though she disapproved she felt herself gazing at it.' 'It' is of course the vivid picture of haggard, handsome Morris Townsend.

 ## Write

Take the extract from *Washington Square* and edit it so that it uses contemporary language and could take place today. You should assume the characters have the same feelings and morals as in the original. The words you change or omit should be only those you *hear* as dated in themselves or in an order (syntax) that isn't how people speak or write today.

Focus points

Chapter 3 looked in detail at what narrative can do within scenes of dialogue. The chapter's main concepts are summarized in the following five points:

- Small bits of narrative can enhance dialogue and develop character, plot and theme in fiction. Identifying narrative – stating who is speaking – is not always necessary. It becomes necessary when a new character speaks or when more than two characters are speaking without identification internal to their speech. Narrative that is descriptive and/or informative can greatly develop plot and theme in scenes of dialogue. It can build in composite to reveal more than is apparent at first reading.

- Writers should use single adverbs appended to identifying narrative very carefully. Such descriptive/informative narrative can easily be cliché. It cannot substitute for emotional expression or tone in the dialogue.

- Writers often use separate clauses or sentences rather than single adverbs or short adverbial phrases to more fully develop the tone and mood of the dialogue, and to intensify the dialogue in ways significant to plot.

- Narrative in dialogue can be very flexible. It can range from third-person omniscience towards an indirect quotation that's close to dialogue. In this way, it can be used to control the pace and tone of the dialogue.

- To avoid problems with single adverbs in characterizing dialogue, you can do without any characterization external to the dialogue or use several more effective ways that make you really say something. Use a specific verb in place of the generic 'said' or 'says'. Use a minor (dependent) clause to modify the identifying narrative. Use a separate sentence of descriptive/informative narrative. Use a separate paragraph to modify the preceding dialogue and/or to develop dialogue that follows. Though these techniques are used by contemporary writers of fiction, most of them have been around for a long time.

Next step

Chapter 4 looks at how dialogue appears in narrative – that is, how dialogue is used in scenes and sections of fiction that are predominantly narrative.

4

Dialogue in narrative

In this chapter you will learn:
- What dialogue in narrative is and how to use it
- About the different ways in which characters can misunderstand dialogue
- About using dialogue in narrative to characterize minor characters or to indicate social mood
- What hypothetical dialogue is.

What is dialogue in narrative?

For the purposes of this book, dialogue in narrative refers to dialogue used in scenes or in sections of scenes that are predominantly narrative.

Here is an example of a bit of dialogue used as a hook into narration at the start of a novel.

> Let me tell you about when I was a girl, our grandfather says.
>
> It is Saturday evening; we always stay at their house on Saturdays. The couch and the chairs are shoved back against the walls. The teak coffee table from the middle of the room is up under the window. The floor has been cleared for backward and forward somersaults, the juggling with oranges and eggs, the how-to-do-a-cartwheel, how-to-stand-on-your-head, how-to-walk-on-your-hands lessons. Our grandfather holds us upside-down by the legs until we get our balance. Our grandfather worked in a circus before he met and married our grandmother. He once did headstands on top of a whole troupe of headstanders. He once walked a tightrope across the Thames. The Thames is a river in London, which is five hundred and twenty-seven miles from here, according to the mileage chart in the RAC book in among our father's books at home.

This is the opening of Ali Smith's novel *Girl Meets Boy*, and that first sentence is dialogue that gets your attention. The narration that follows is excellent, but you start reading it with the promise of that first line of dialogue in mind, that story about when grandfather was a girl.

 Key idea

A short statement of dialogue can bring life – character and energy – into narrative.

Sometimes such dialogue statements are compared to spice added to flavour a dish. This isn't a good comparison because it suggests that a writer has written some bland narrative and has then gone back to add just the right touch of dialogue. As a matter of fact, it's nonsense – it's not how writers work. It could be that Ali Smith wrote the opening just as it stands; it could be that she wrote the narrative paragraph first and then thought to write the dialogue or to move the dialogue as it now reads. In any case, like any serious writer, she was trying to write her best at all times. Writers do not think, 'Oh this is only narrative (or dialogue), so I'll coast along at half-effort until some dialogue (or narrative) to *really* start writing.' Writing is not like painting by numbers. (Neither, of course, is painting.) Even if the writer is fully aware of the power of the attention-getting dialogue, it more likely becomes a spur to keep the energy and liveliness going in the following narrative. So while there's no doubt the opening dialogue is a hook to readers' interest, it doesn't make good readers skip over the following narrative to get to what appears to be the transgendered story the grandfather promises. In fact, the spirit of this dialogue continues into the narrative's somersaults and juggling and cartwheels and in the grandfather working in the circus doing not mere headstands but headstands atop 'a whole troupe of headstanders'.

As well as standing alone before narrative, dialogue can also be incorporated within a paragraph that is substantially narration. The following paragraph is from my novel *Stealing Home*. It occurs during a scene of seduction. The narrator, to this point, has avoided responding to the flirtatious behaviour of Anita, his childhood acquaintance and a married woman. The scene takes place in Belize.

> Lord's Bar inside was a pleasant surprise. Cool air conditioning. Smoothed concrete walls painted in tans and shades of red. Black lacquer chairs and tables, a bandstand, and a long back-mirrored bar that wouldn't look out of place in Rockefeller Plaza. 'Nice,' Anita said. I said, 'Nice. Drug money.' The place was empty except for a couple at the bar. We went and sat a few seats away and ordered rum punch. The drinks came in large bowl glasses. Perfect rum punch, peppered with fresh nutmeg and light to taste but strong. We toasted our coming trip, drank and went silent.
>
> We were looking in the mirror at the other couple. They were very fine looking, a black couple sitting to Anita's side. I saw the man glance at Anita's legs. Her dress sat high on her crossed thighs. We ordered more rum punch. Anita leaned into me and whispered, 'See the four of us in the mirror? They have darker skins, but we look more African.' I looked in the mirror. In a way she was right: her heavy lips and long almond eyes, and I thought I might pass for a pale Ethiopian. The man kept glancing at Anita. I was sure he could see her pants. I wondered if she knew that. When the drinks came, Anita toasted: 'To the four of us,' and laughed.

Ordinarily, I use the convention of marking a change of speaker by a new paragraph. I don't remember how aware I was on first writing this of wanting to keep the bits of dialogue within the narrative paragraph. But looking at it now in the context of this scene, I see how it works.

Anita and the narrator have just come into the bar from dangerous streets in a city they don't know at all. So the sense of relative safety is present in the *containment* of their dialogue in the narrative. At the same time, it is the feeling engendered by the place and its other two customers that dominates my main-character couple's consciousness, and their dialogue is a direct verbal response to the stimulus of the setting described in narrative. What unites narrative and dialogue is the sense of growing sexual excitement. The descriptive narration – first-person point of view – reflects this in its pace, some of which is near telegram style. And, aside of Anita's comment about looking more African themselves than the black couple, the bits of dialogue in the paragraph are short, clipped and speedy. It's worth saying that once they leave the bar and are out walking the streets, the pace of narrative and dialogue slows down again, only accelerating when, in a restaurant, the narrator finally gives in to his desire for Anita.

Focus point

The conventions of dialogue are not rigid rules. They should be modified, even broken, when doing so makes for better writing.

Write

Find a likely paragraph of narrative in your own writing and add one or two bits of dialogue within it that enhance the scene or setting or mood or characterizations – the content – of the paragraph.

Case study: Ian McEwan, *On Chesil Beach*

Ian McEwan's novel *On Chesil Beach* opens with a sentence that pretty well sums up its subject: 'They were young, educated, and both virgins on their wedding night, and they lived in a time when a conversation about sexual difficulties was plainly impossible.'

Sexual problems as the central mover of plot is more typically the stuff of comic novels, but McEwan tells the story from the couple's points of view, and it is sad and moving, because it's hardly the fault of either that their sexual innocence becomes, in action, their sexual ignorance, and this so baffles their ordinary feelings and intelligence that they say what they don't quite mean since they don't at all know how to say such things, and they mishear what is said because they have no experience with which to interpret it. They certainly are in love as much as most people who are virgins, that is, before the intense bonding of full sexual passion. This is a fine, quiet novel which creates deep reader pity.

This is a quiet novel.

One reason for its quiet is the cool, clear tone of the narrative. This changes only when shifting to one or other of Edward's and Florence's point of view during times of anxiety, confusion or anger. The other reason for its quiet is that there's not much dialogue in the novel, remarkably little, in fact. (Maybe this only becomes obvious if you're writing a book on how to write dialogue. I assumed this would have been noted by reviewers of the novel and interviewers of its writer, but my research found no mention of this significant absence of dialogue in any of the reviews/interviews I have managed to find.)

The novel – or novella (around 40,000 words) – is divided into five parts. Part One across its 30 pages contains no scenes of dialogue and eight lines of dialogue. Part Two, with 38 pages, has one page of dialogue and five other lines of dialogue. In Part Three's 28 pages there are eight lines of dialogue, two of them consisting of only one word during a long narrative scene. Part Four contains two lines of dialogue in 24 pages. It is only in the final Part Five that there is an extended scene of dialogue, taking up 15 of the 27 pages.

This silence isn't typical of McEwan's fiction. He generally writes in a mix of narrative and dialogue within the range of most writers. Some of his work, like *Atonement*, is rich in dialogue. So why has he chosen (and 'chosen' here means 'ended up with') to have so little dialogue?

The obvious reason is that Edward and Florence can't speak to each other – not about the botched sexuality at the centre of the story.

It's worth looking in some detail at the scattered lines of dialogue, 'scattered' only in the sense of physically separated. They are anything but random.

In the present time of the novel, from the couple's wedding day to the morning after, Part One goes from the couple's arrival after the wedding and reception at the hotel until they finish their dinner in the honeymoon suite and go into the bedroom.

Ten pages into the book, after finishing their first course, a slice of melon with a glazed cherry (the cherry doubtless out of a bottle, the melon doubtless unripe) stuck onto it for some glamour, Edward, 'with an ironic flourish', has offered his cherry to his bride. Florence has accepted it, 'letting him see her tongue, conscious that in flirting with him like this she would be making matters worse for herself.' Edward then asks the local boys serving as waiters for another:

'Any more of these things?'

'Ain't none, sir. Sorry sir.'

This, the novel's first dialogue, reads comically in its mismatches of occasion with reality, middle-class attempt to be just one of the lads, and a reply of nervous formality – one of the actual lads attempting to be one of the gents – raucously perfect, from the glass-breaking 'Ain't' to the perfect ear that puts in that second 'sir' after the 'Sorry'. So far, so Waugh.

But there's more to it. It isn't just the stuff of a best man's bad wedding speech. There is Florence's fear of the problems facing her in accepting Edward's romantic/mock-romantic gesture. What's more, all this business, including the writer's decision to start the characters talking, is over a cherry. The not-so-buried pun of cherry as 'virginity' is bitter. Edward has offered Florence his cherry, but she has not offered Edward hers. It is only at the end of this scene that the reader can fully understand this.

The next dialogue, after six pages of narrative in which among other aspects of the lead-up to their marriage, we learn of Florence's extreme physical self-consciousness causing her to be extremely awkward, except in playing music, is the three words she speaks as their main course is served: 'Here it comes.' Florence is only referring to the food being served. But in the context of the ensuing scene, this takes on a larger and, for her, more ominous meaning, something like: Here comes the ritual sacrifice of my body, the brute violence of male penetration, the end of my privacy and modesty.

There is no further dialogue for nine pages. They are left alone with their heavy meal of beef, the sound of waves, and the view of the beach from the windows. And their manners, which are the manners of their time, make them sit and pretend to want to eat supper while snatches of the news come to them from the radio in the hotel sitting room below. Edward's thoughts shift back and forth between the politics on the radio and thoughts of being in bed with Florence. He feels stifled and frustrated that they both seem unable to talk to each other on their wedding night. He has to break the awful chains of silence by saying something.

'We could go downstairs and listen properly.'

He hoped he was being humorous, directing his sarcasm against them both, but his words emerged with surprising ferocity, and Florence blushed. She thought he was criticising her for preferring the wireless to him, and before he could soften or lighten his remark she said, hurriedly, 'Or we could go and lie on the bed,' and nervously swiped an invisible hair from her forehead. To demonstrate how wrong he was, she was proposing what she knew he most wanted and she dreaded.

Note how the writer breaks with the convention of having Florence's speech on a new paragraph. Her speech is much more hemmed in by the context of the narrative paragraph. Note, too, that without the narrative, the two lines of dialogue, written together, would give a very different meaning:

'We could go downstairs and listen properly.'

'Or we could go and lie on the bed.'

Although this could be how the words were spoken in 'real' time, the dialogue as it is embedded in the narrative is completely different. It sets the pattern for the tension under which they speak, the pattern for the misunderstandings between them which grow from this point on. It works something like this. Their internal tensions cause them to begin speaking with more emotion than they intend. By failing to control the tone, each is naturally misinterpreted by the other. This causes the reactive response to be further from what they mean or desire. Edward's tension makes his statement – intended only as light humour to break the silence – come out 'with surprising ferocity'. This makes Florence interpret his words as a rebuke to her for 'preferring the wireless to him' (it wasn't a rebuke; they both listened in embarrassed silence), and in trying to put right her understanding of what Edward means – a misunderstanding, though natural enough considering how his words *sounded* – she replies with what she assumes is the show of love he wants from her. Lying on the bed is not only what she doesn't want but, at this point, not what Edward was getting at. His outburst was, pathetically, an attempt to make normal, polite conversation, something to break the strangulating silence.

It is this pattern of understandable (to the reader) misunderstandings between the couple that makes their growing frustration so pitiful. And that it's pity rather than amusement the reader feels is controlled by the informative narration. Both characters, says the narrative, feel worse and worse, more and more baffled and angered by the other's reactions and responses, as the scene goes on.

This means that such scenes don't need much dialogue but do need the writer to interpret for the reader what is going on emotionally and in the characters' thoughts during the long silences between dialogue. The long silences themselves become part of the characterization and of the action within these scenes of extensive narration. And even if, as imagined above, the last two quoted lines of dialogue were spoken with no pause between them in the 'real' time of the scene, the writer's insertion of the narrative between them creates the sense of the character's tense, awkward silence and essential inability to communicate deep misgivings about sexuality.

At this point in the scene, still at the table, Edward misinterprets Florence's suggestion as a wonderful change in her attitude to sex, and he puts it down to her new status as a married woman. She, however, feels he must see her smile for what it is – completely artificial; he actually sees her as more beautiful than ever.
'You're very beautiful,' he whispered.

She made herself remember how much she loved this man. He was kind, sensitive, he loved her and could do her no harm. She shrugged herself deeper into his embrace, close against his chest, and inhaled his familiar scent, which had a woody quality and was reassuring.
'I'm so happy here with you.'
'I'm so happy too,' she said quietly.

When they kissed she immediately felt his tongue, tensed and strong, pushing past her teeth, like some bully shouldering his way into a room. Entering her. Her own tongue folded and recoiled in automatic distaste, making even more space for Edward. He knew well enough she did not like this kind of kissing, and he had never before been so assertive. With his lips clamped firmly onto hers, he probed the fleshy floor of her mouth, then moved round inside the teeth of her lower jaw to the empty place where three years ago a wisdom tooth had crookedly grown until removed under general anaesthesia. This cavity was where her own tongue usually strayed when she was lost in thought. By association, it was more like an idea than a location, a private, imaginary place rather than a hollow in her gum, and it seemed peculiar to her that another tongue should be able to go there too. It was the hard tapering tip of this alien muscle, quiveringly alive, that repelled her.

The potential for direct, simple happiness glimpsed in the two lines of dialogue is immediately stifled. She feels his tongue in her mouth 'like some bully'. It is 'Entering her'. Her tongue does what her entire being does: it 'recoiled in automatic distaste'. Edward continues boldly. Her suggestion of lying on the bed has led to his 'never before being so assertive', even though he knows she doesn't like being kissed like this. What follows is narrative description of such dry anatomical precision as to totally unsex the action. And when the gap of the removed wisdom tooth is described, the scene teeters for a moment at the edge of comedy ('it seemed peculiar to her that another tongue should be able to go there too'). But the narrative immediately draws back into repulsion, and the troubles – the sad conflict – continue to grow.

These misunderstandings through the dialogue are extended into the action of subsequent narrative. With Edward's tongue still in her mouth, Florence thinks of what her marriage actually means – that she has agreed to this primitive rite of her husband to sexually penetrate her, his tongue being only 'a small scale enactment, a ritual *tableau vivant*, of what was still to come'. These thoughts so revolt her that 'now she really did think she was going to be sick'.

Edward, hearing her suppressed retching, believes Florence is moaning with pleasure, and he 'knew that his happiness was almost complete'. In this way, both dialogue and narrative become a series of complete disconnects.

Part Three of the novel ends with the debacle of the wedding night; the first section of Part Four recounts the year between the couple's meeting and their marriage. In one of its scenes, since Florence is a violinist dedicated to creating and leading a string quartet, Edward, who hasn't known classical music, attends a rehearsal and begins to be moved by the music. He responds by bringing Florence some of his favourite rock and roll records. She tries but can't, after all, see the point of such simple, thumping, crashing rhythm.

...He kissed her and told her she was the squarest person in all of Western civilisation.

'But you love me,' she said.

'*Therefore* I love you.'

This, the first dialogue in 17 pages, is intended and taken as romantic gallantry on Edward's part. And there is no doubt that he's called her 'the squarest' affectionately. Yet the reader, knowing how disastrously the wedding night has gone (and not yet knowing what follows that night, which makes up the final section of Part Four), has to understand this exchange with dark irony.

For Florence has turned out to truly be 'the squarest' in not appreciating sex, as well as rock and roll. Her musical aversion, for that matter, is particularly significant, since the relentless loud, thumping, simple rhythm of rock and roll is nothing if not the aural equivalent of copulative rhythm. The actual name of the music 'rock and roll' comes from 'rocking and rolling', a black American expression for sex. It's little wonder that Florence can't take to this music, even if she – as opposed to the reader – isn't able to realize the physical and emotional depth of her aversion. And in this respect, the gallantry of Edward's emphasis, '*Therefore* I love you,' is an even more pathetic irony.

 Key idea

Dialogue in narrative can be important in the development of character and plot. It requires the context of well-written narrative.

 Write

Write a two- to three-page, two-character scene essentially presented through narrative in which the people meet for the first time, perhaps having to share a table in a restaurant or a park bench. One of them is immediately attracted to the other, but the attraction isn't mutual. Using a minimum of dialogue, as in the Case study above, make the characters' reaction to each other result in both of them misunderstanding what the other means. This may also involve the dialogue statements coming out not quite as the speaker intends. You should first decide on the tone you intend for the scene. Is it to be comic? Sad? Fantastic? (Note: If you have a novel or short story MS with a scene you think might benefit from this sort of revision, by all means use that instead.)

 Focus point

Effective dialogue in narrative – as well as in scenes of dialogue – can be structured on misunderstandings of what is said.

Can dialogue in narrative be misunderstood by characters *despite* what is being said?

Short answer: certainly.

Dialogue in narrative can of course be misunderstood, as what people say in real life can be heard but misunderstood for several sorts of reasons.

Some of the reasons may be a result of the listener not knowing the speaker very well. Sixteen-year-old Robbie, known by his family and close friends to be lazy in action but obliging in speech, may be taken literally by Mrs Bracken, a neighbour, when he offers to help her clear out the junk that's collected in her garage this coming Saturday. Or the speaker may be a congenital health fabulist (a hypochondriac) who the listener believes can't have more than months to live, not knowing that he's been telling the same stories now for 35 years.

Or a speaker may be lying, or knowingly telling only half the truth, or consciously distorting certain aspects of the subject. Such intentional misinformation, if believed, may be what the speaker wishes, but it is still a misunderstanding of the *nature* of what has been spoken on the part of the listener. On the other hand, teenager Robbie may actually believe, at the time he offers his help, that he's actually going to do it.

Another variation is the misunderstanding due to second- or third-hand imprecision, the distortion typical of gossip. Its reception by listeners is dependent on their nature and their regard for the speaker.

A common cause of misunderstanding by the listener is an inability to identify the speaker's tone, such as the failure to pick up the irony in what's said. This can be the result of the listener having a more literal way of speaking and hearing. And this, in turn, can be due to different family and/or educational background than the speaker.

Another type of misunderstanding arises when the listener, from experience of or information about the speaker, assumes that the speaker's words are not to be trusted when in this instance the speaker is telling the truth (the-boy-who-cried-wolf example). If readers are aware of this when the inveterate liar/joker speaks, they understand the irony in the situation. The writer might also present it so that readers only learn later of the truth of the statement and its implications.

As you've seen, these and other types of misunderstandings can arise in the smallest dialogues within narrative scenes. Obviously, they also occur is dialogue scenes.

What are other effects of dialogue in narrative?

Dialogue in narrative can be useful as an identifying characteristic, or 'marker', for minor characters.

Alan's father was one of those staunch Labour Party supporters who saw no contradiction in also being a supporter of the British Empire. From the late 1940s through the 1960s, as the map of the world was drained of its imperial red, he kept complaining that it was foolish to give up country after country because they would only, one way or another, fall into the hands of the Yanks. From then on, for the rest of his long life, he viewed all American success overseas from the perspective of a disgruntled colonialist. An American oil contract in the Middle East? He'd say, 'We handed it to the damn Yanks!' An award at the Cannes Film Festival for a Hollywood movie? 'We handed it to the damn Yanks!' Alan remembered watching an Olympic award ceremony on TV when the gold went to the USA and the bronze to the UK. He'd turned to his father and asked how that was supposed to be related to losing India and Rhodesia? His father shook his head, muttered about not being sure, and then said, 'But we handed it to the damn Yanks!'

It's the direct speech which helps emphasize and make memorable Alan's father, a secondary character. Alan, a main character, needs no special marking by such a device since he's developed in both dialogue and narrative throughout the piece of fiction.

Another use of a line or so of dialogue in a narrative scene can be thought of as the occasional voice. Such short bursts of dialogue help develop the mood of the setting through which main characters 'move' in the plot. They can be subjectively memorable in the main characters in that they support such a state, or they may be voices that ironically counter that state of mind. The sales attendant's 'Glad to be of help' or 'I have no more time to waste: do you want to buy it or not?' are in these instances not really markers of the salesperson as much as indicators of social mood affecting more realized characters.

 Key idea

Dialogue in narrative can create memorable markers for minor characters and indicators of social mood as context for major and minor characters.

Write

Write a short narrative scene in which you describe a minor character important to a main character and give her/him a characteristic bit of 'marker' dialogue.

Write another short narrative scene in which you imagine your character out and about and in a particular mood or state – in a rush, happy, grieving, etc. – and in an exchange with someone she/he doesn't personally know, giving this someone a short statement of dialogue which in some way, positively or negatively, 'gets' to your character.

What is hypothetical dialogue?

Hypothetical dialogue is dialogue that usually occurs with narration of a character's thought, or, for first-person narration, within the character's thoughts. It may, in part, have occurred, but its main purpose is to put forward an argument in direct speech.

> You might think this is rubbish – preachy, self-justificatory rubbish. You might think that I behaved towards Veronica like a typically callow male, and that all my 'conclusions' are reversible. For instance, 'After we broke up, she slept with me' flips easily into 'After she slept with me, I broke up with her.' You might also decide...'

Julian Barnes, The Sense of an Ending

Here, Tony, the narrator-character is rehearsing the possible interpretations, misinterpretations and reinterpretations of his actions in the distant past. He has already acknowledged that his own memory may have changed over the years about what exactly took place. What the writer wanted for his character at this point was to have the reader hear Tony's voice giving these two reversed statements. Since the reader is constantly 'hearing' Tony narrate, giving two dialogue statements breaks the pattern enough for the reader to 'hear' in a different way. Making a point like this is also within the realistic style of this novel, as people certainly do 'talk to themselves' from time to time within their thinking.

Write

Write a narrative of one or two paragraphs which contains several statements of hypothetical dialogue. The dialogue might be used to make a point developed in the narrative or to question/challenge that point.

Focus points

Chapter 4 looked at a variety of functions for statements of dialogue in the context of essentially narrative writing. Its main ideas are summarized in the following five points:

- Dialogue in narrative refers to dialogue used in scenes or sections of scenes that are primarily narrative. Such short dialogue statements bring life – character and energy – into narrative. As always, such dialogue shows rather than tells.
- Dialogue can be incorporated into a paragraph which is predominantly narrative, breaking the convention of a new paragraph to mark a change of speaker, when the writer wants the dialogue to be a close part of narrative in tone, mood or content.
- Dialogue can occur in narrative sections of fiction when the meaning of the dialogue is dependent on the narrative's explanations of the often complex emotions and intentions of the speakers. Such dialogue may take on special intensity because of its infrequency.
- Dialogue in narrative may be based on misunderstandings and can continue to create further misunderstandings. The characters' confusion may grow, but generally the narrative explains the confusion for the reader.
- Dialogue in narrative may also be used to create 'markers' for minor characters; these are spoken expressions to make these characters vivid and memorable. Hypothetical dialogue in sections of narrative is used to develop or counter a narrative argument. It imitates a form of thinking but shifts to a direct voice.

Next step

The last three chapters of the book looked at how dialogue works to present character, how narrative works to modify dialogue, and how dialogue can be used in scenes and sections of fiction where narrative dominates. Chapter 5 focuses on the different formats in which dialogue can be presented.

5

Versions of dialogue

In this chapter you will learn:

- About different ways of presenting dialogue
- How letters can create the effect of dialogue
- How journals and diaries can be used to present dialogue
- How telephone dialogue can reveal character.

This chapter looks at the main versions or formats in which dialogue can be presented other than as direct dialogue as discussed in the three previous chapters. It's worth remembering as you read this chapter that it is not an academic survey of a subsection of fiction as literature. It's a practical presentation of the various formats you can use to present (to represent) dialogue. Some of the ways are very old, some are very new, all are potentially very useful to your writing.

While it's obvious that dialogue can be presented in letters, can letters themselves be regarded as dialogue?

Short answer: no, and in some ways yes.

As dialogue in fiction is defined to be the representation in writing of people *speaking*, letters in fiction as the representation of people *writing* cannot be dialogue.

Nevertheless, fiction is a set of conventions, constantly changing yet just as constantly incorporating past conventions found to be useful to writers. One of the earliest of these conventions is that of the novel written entirely as a series of letters between characters and as a journal kept by the central letter-writing character. The earliest of these novels, *Pamela*, by Samuel Richardson, was published in 1740 and was a sensational success. This may in part have been due to the fact that at that time the novel-reading public was pretty much the same as the letter-writing public, an educated minority with at least some money to spend on books, and they were delighted to read a story that used the same written form they used to communicate with friends and family, as well as in domestic and business affairs.

Here is the title-page text of the original edition:

PAMELA

OR

VIRTUE REWARDED

In a SERIES of

FAMILIAR LETTERS

FROM A

Beautiful Young Damsel,

> To her PARENTS
> Now first Published
> In order to cultivate the Principles of
> VIRTUE and RELIGION in the Minds of
> the YOUTH of BOTH SEXES

The moralistic insistence of the book (somewhat at odds with the steely-minded heroine) may have also made it more palatable to the parents 'of the youth of both sexes' who were footing the bill for the book. Moreover, it might have been a relief for them to see such a proper title page as opposed to those like that of a novel published in 1722 by Daniel Defoe.

> THE
> FORTUNES & MISFORTUNES
> OF THE FAMOUS
> MOLL FLANDERS
> &C.
> who was born in Newgate,
> and during a life of continued variety
> for three-score years beside her childhood,
> was twelve years a whore,
> five times a wife,
> (whereof once to her own brother)
> twelve years a thief,
> eight year a transported felon
> in Virginia,
> at last grew rich, and
> died a penitent.
> WRITTEN FROM HER OWN MEMORANDUMS

Richardson's pioneer letter novel, like those that followed, is not only reproducing the more formal letter writing of the time but, in its more informal sections, *is writing in the voice of the character writing*, so that it reads to us, as well as to its original readers, more like direct speech – like dialogue. Personal letter writing was to eighteenth-century communication something like telephoning is to twentieth- and twenty-first-century communication.

Certainly, the formal letter sections don't seem much like ordinary speech. Here's the opening of *Pamela*:

LETTER 1

Dear Father and Mother,

I have great trouble, and some comfort, to acquaint you with. The trouble is, that my good lady died of the illness I mentioned to you, and left us all much grieved for the loss of her; for she was a dear good lady, and kind to all us her servants. Much I feared that as I was taken by her ladyship to wait upon her person, I should be quite destitute again, and forced to return to you and my poor mother, who have enough to do to maintain yourselves; and as my lady's goodness had put me to write and cast accounts, and made me a little expert at my needle, and otherwise qualified above my degree, it was not every family that could have found a place that your poor Pamela was fit for; but God, whose graciousness to us we have so often experienced at a pinch, put it into my good lady's heart, on her death-bed, just an hour before she expired, to recommend to my young master all her servants, one by one; and when it came to my turn to be recommended, (for I was sobbing and crying at her pillow) she could only say, My dear son! – and so broke off a little; and then recovering – Remember my poor Pamela – And these were some of her last words! O how my eyes run – Don't wonder to see the paper so blotted.

The letter begins formally, but once it gets to the dialogue of the dying mistress, Pamela's emotions are released, so that by the end of the extract – 'And these were some of her last words! O how my eyes run – Do not wonder to see the paper so blotted' – this reads and sounds much more like dialogue.

The letter ends formally with:

I know, dear father and mother, I must give you both grief and pleasure; and so I will only say, Pray for your Pamela; who will ever be

Your most dutiful Daughter

But it suddenly continues with:

I have been scared out of my senses; for just now, as I was folding up this letter in my late lady's dressing-room, in comes

my young master! Good sirs! how was I frightened! I went to
hide the letter in my bosom; and he, seeing me tremble, said,
smiling, To whom have you been writing, Pamela? – I said, in my
confusion, Pray your honour forgive me! – Only to my father
and mother. He said, Well then, let me see how you are come on
in your writing! O how ashamed I was! – He took it, without
saying more, and read it quite through, and then gave it me
again…

And the reader hears the girl talking to her parents.

> ## Key idea
>
> Letters can give the effect of dialogue if they substantially
> reproduce the direct speech of the character writing them.

> ## Write
>
> Choosing a character you've already created, have her/him write
> a personal letter of one or two pages that captures the character's
> speaking voice.

How do letters heard by the reader as the voice of a character differ from direct dialogue?

One approach to understanding the difference is to think of an
exchange of letters in character voices as a series of alternating
monologues with a gap of time between each. No other voice
interrupts the letter writer. They write as much as they want and do
not have to consider the reactions of the recipient-listener as they do
so. In practice, however, the letter writer often does acknowledge or
anticipate reactions and incorporates this into the letter, if only to
explain why a choice has been or will be made despite the objections
of the recipient. This is the 'despite you always warning me to stay
away from Paul, I find him sensitive and intuitive'. This can also be
the 'I know you'll be delighted to hear that I've finally gone back to
college to finish my BA.'

Although the gap between letters radically slows the receipt of feedback as compared with ordinary dialogue, it offers you the fiction writer useful possibilities. For one, the response letter can solve, create or change problems posed by the letter sent. That is, significant events (plot) can have taken place in the interval between sending the letter and receiving the response. When you think of it, in a story or novel composed entirely of letters, events generally happen off scene. They may happen simultaneously with the letter writing, as in: 'As I write, the furniture is being taken from the house, and I'm trying to be brave, but honestly it's breaking my heart.' If the events happen before the letter writing, they can provide a sense of anticipation in your reader. If the writing is good (and that's the default assumption of this book), your reader, like the fictional letter recipient, awaits the next letter with real interest, be that in hope, anxiety or dread, or just as good gossip.

The time gap can also give the letter writer the opportunity to find out more about the subject driving the story. In the eponymous Pamela's case, this involves the actions of her young master and her interpretations of these actions. Pamela's overuse of exclamation marks, by the way, is one of the author's most convincing imitations of realistic personal letters – from that day to this. It isn't formal grammar and punctuation you're after in writing any form of dialogue, it's the grammar and punctuation that best recreate the 'real' voice you want. Those exclamation marks are the spicing of real letters and emails, or maybe the ketchup and HP sauce.

The chief consideration when writing letters in your fiction that manage to carry the voice of the character who's writing is: Would your character be able to write a letter in that way? For while you, the author, may be able to, you have to test the feasibility of such a letter against your character's writing ability, not your own.

Many people, even in the days when personal letter writing was much more prevalent and frequent than today, could not write 'natural-sounding' letters, could not write as they spoke. This was and is not a question of the person's education or general ability to write fairly clearly and coherently. The truth seems to be that few people have the talent or lack of self-consciousness to write like they speak. Some fiction writers are good at it because they do so much writing in their own and other people's voices that writing to family or friends isn't a particularly self-conscious act. Others, like visual artists, in my experience, can write this sort of letter. As in their speech, visual imagery comes easily to them out of their working practice, and they apply this to personal letter or email writing, evoking emotional states and writing descriptively with enviable ease.

Yet the challenge seems well worth taking up, especially if your character speaks in a particularly striking way. On the other hand, if such a vivid speaker wouldn't bother to write a letter, you can't force it. But you will find that some characters who can't write a letter in a real voice can do it in a note.

Key idea

Sometimes characters can dash off a note that sounds like dialogue when they couldn't do it in a letter.

It might go like this:

Bobby,

I've left supper ready for you to reheat and if you don't eat the vegetables you'd better go out and bury them somewhere off the property because I'm going to check out everywhere else when I get back and if I find a trace of you dumping them you'll really really wish you ate them.

Love, Mom

PS: Don't even dream of saying the dog ate them. Rollo's with me!

Focus point

Letters can sound like dialogue, but they have to be plausible as written by your character.

Write

Choose three of your characters and have them write an informal note to a family member, a friend, or someone they know well at work. Are any of them able to write it in 'dialogue voice'?

How are journals and diaries used in fiction to present dialogue?

Journals, like diaries, have dated entries. Unlike diaries, they are not intended to be kept every day. Both formats can include the recording of direct dialogue. In general, diary entries tend to be shorter, recording what happened each day, while journals have longer entries which are often subject based. Their observations may be developed into shorter or longer essays. Diaries are of two sorts: the absolutely private diary intended for no one's eyes but the writer's (the discovery of which by someone else has become a plot cliché) and those, like war diaries, sometimes intended for later perusal by others or for publication. Diaries, like journals, have been around for a long time. The seventeenth century saw a proliferation of journals of exploration and discovery published, some accurate, others clearly fabulous. By the start of the eighteenth century, writers were satirizing such wild, invented stories, and *Gulliver's Travels* is in format a satire on such tall traveller's tales. Journals were sometimes written by people of some eminence with an eye to publication.

With this journal-reading public in mind, Daniel Defoe in 1722 published *A Journal of the Plague Year*, a fiction purporting to be non-fiction. This was nothing like the fantastic inventions of false traveller's tales. What's fictional is that the eyewitness didn't exist: Defoe was four years old in the plague year of 1665. Though entries aren't dated – it's written in a continuous format – weekly death tolls are given to mark the progress of time and the plague, and the narrative is so full of specific, accurate detail, that readers who remembered the plague took it to be the account of an eyewitness. It is full of lists, numbers and locations named by London borough and street. In it, Defoe tells a moral story of three brothers who were unable to flee London, and he begins their dialogue directly:

> Says John the Biscuit Baker, one Day to Thomas his brother, the Sail Maker, Brother Tom, what will become of us? The Plague grows hot in the City, and encreases this way: What shall we do?

> Truly, says Thomas, I am at a great loss what to do, for I find, if it comes down into Wapping, I shall be turn'd out of my lodging...

And then Defoe uses the theatrical convention of identifying dialogue:

John: Turn'd out of your Lodging, Tom? If you are, I don't know who will take you in; for People are so afraid of one another now, there's no getting a lodging anywhere.

Tho.: Why? The People where I lodge are good civil People, and have kindness enough for me too...

This dialogue scene continues for pages. Right from the start of fiction in English, the journal format was used and dialogue was incorporated.

Richardson's *Pamela*, perhaps influenced by Defoe or some of the other real or pretend journals, includes the journal format. After 32 letters between Pamela and her parents, the last of which tells us she has been taken away to her young master's country property and is there being kept a virtual prisoner, Pamela begins keeping a journal. Richardson's minutely detailed table of contents describes the journal as 'Begun for her amusement, and in her hopes to find some opportunity to send it to them [her parents]. Describes the servants there. All her hopes centre in moving Mr. Williams [a local clergyman] to assist her escape.'

So Pamela becomes the narrator of this dated-entry section of the novel which itself contains dialogue as well as letters.

From the earliest days of fiction, writers were using a number of existing 'real' (non-fiction) forms to present their stories in the belief that they would help make their work more believable. Though Richardson's younger contemporaries found *Pamela* quite unbelievable, as did Henry Fielding who parodied the novel in *Shamela*, it was because of its stultifyingly moralistic tone of the writing and not because of its letter and journal formats.

Those formats remain very much in fashion, as witnessed by the deserved success of Helen Fielding's *Bridget Jones's Diary* and Sue Townsend's instant classic *The Secret Diary of Adrian Mole, Aged 13¾*.

In A. S. Byatt's novel *Possession*, published in 1990, the letter and journal formats are among those used to create the research which brings together the book's two present-day protagonists in their discovery of the secret love affair between two mid-Victorian poets and writers. In addition to Victorian journals and letters, the fiction and poetry of these writers and modern literary criticism concerning them is presented as the primary and secondary sources of the contemporary research and discovery. The contemporary and the Victorian voices presented through this range of formats make a counterpart to the direct dialogue between the two present-day researchers as they become caught up in the passionate love affair their work uncovers, caught up as well in their own growing romance. This range of voices and formats energizes the novel's structure and becomes as much a part of the 'showing' of the writing – in dialogue and action – as are the scenes between the living characters.

Write

At some point, it could be useful for you to create your own Case study by reading *Possession* to see how a range of dialogue formats can be integrated with plot, character and theme – the central elements of fiction.

Key idea

The vividness provided by dialogue can be extended into a variety of prose formats.

How revealing of character can telephone dialogue be?

Focus point

Telephone conversation in all its varieties is a format of pure dialogue.

Telephone conversations began to appear in fiction as soon as telephones began to appear in homes and businesses. The early fictional phone conversations were typically about conveying information vital to story and plot development. This was doubtless a reflection of the earliest telephone use which was substantially utilitarian. So news of accidents, changes of plans, times of meetings and the like made up the content. As telephone use became ubiquitous, fiction reflected conversations made for pleasure, for keeping in touch, and all the other personal reasons for calling, including the mundane need to hear another human voice. The subsequent inventions of answerphone/voicemail and voice messaging extended the variety of telephonic dialogue.

Following on from the Focus point above, telephone dialogue can be as revealing of character as you want to make it. In itself, there's no supporting narrative, but, of course, that could be added.

You could write an entire novel as a series of telephone conversations and messages, or even as one long continuous conversation, perhaps of dialogues within dialogue, or as a voice message, which would in effect be a novel as monologue, basically a first-person narration. You can imagine a recording device set for a day rather than for seconds. This is somewhat akin to Philip Roth's *Portnoy's Complaint*, which appears to be a patient talking to an analyst who has all the time in the world to listen, until the last line in the novel reveals that the patient has yet to say a word. The point is that no fictional use of the telephone for dialogue is out of bounds – as long as it works.

It will be obvious from your own experience that some people seem natural telephone talkers while others are not. This isn't necessarily related to how gabby or close-mouthed they are in the flesh. So your decisions about how to present your character on the telephone involve the same complex of factors you take into consideration in presenting them in any dialogue form.

Key idea

The single distinction between telephone and fact-to-face dialogue is the physical separation. The speakers don't see each other's physical cues to emotions; they only hear them. Accompanying narrative must take this into account.

Case study: Irving Weinman, *Wolf Tones*

The following Case study, the only one in this chapter, involves extensive extracting to trace the development and its feedback into the writer's thinking of the use of the telephone.

My novel *Wolf Tones* is the story of what happens to Ethan Baum, a young writer who leaves his home town of Boston to try to start a new life in New Mexico. His marriage has failed, his affair with a graduate student has failed, and after early success with novels he has serious writer's block. Moreover, he has serious problems with his difficult father, a man he believes he adores and who has a calming influence on him, a famous philosopher who lives and works in Boston. Of course he takes his problems with him. But, from this distance, he's able to begin to get a bit of objectivity on his relationship with his father.

The novel is narrated in the third person, present tense, with omniscience limited to Ethan's point of view. There are flashbacks throughout the novel, but in the present tense Ethan's father Meyer Baum appears only as a voice over the telephone or answerphone. This wasn't an idea I had in making preliminary notes for the novel or when I started writing. But fairly early in writing the first draft, I knew Meyer would probably not appear, though it took me longer to understand why.

The first telephone call from Meyer to Ethan comes at the start of the first chapter, when Ethan is asleep with a hangover in a cheap Albuquerque motel. The night before, he's attended a faculty party and, drunk, managed to brawl with the host, break his nose, and wake up hours later back at his motel with the man's wife in his bed. There she informs him her husband is Ethan's boss in the university teaching job he's about to begin.

His eyes open. His ears ring. It's the telephone. Lucy's smell is still in his bed, yet the entire night is unbelievable. He picks up the phone. 'Ethan? It's seven-thirty your time. I wanted to make sure I caught you. You said you'd call when you arrived. I've been thinking about my funeral.'

Ethan says, 'Good morning, Meyer,' to his father, the philosopher Meyer Baum, who occasionally revises the details of his funeral. Ethan sighs, without thinking why.

His father continues: 'Small, I'm thinking now, by invitation only. Even family. Especially family by invitation only.'

Ethan says, 'Will I be among the invited?'
'Who do you imagine will send the invitations? I'm thinking small not only because throwing the funeral open would give so many people the opportunity of not attending, but also to reduce the chance that the wrong grouping would turn up and that the Meyer Baum they'd – what's the word here, Ethan: evoke, concoct, apostrophize, effigize – is there a verb from effigy? – would be so little like how I see myself as to be grotesque. Worse, slightly farcical. And I mean regardless if this concoction were better or worse than the so-called "real" me. Why didn't you call?'

Because of this, thinks Ethan, because you haven't said hello or asked how I am, because…

He says, 'I had a strange night. One moment there was a full moon, the next, there was no moon. Yet the sky was cloudless. That's something about out here, the clear night.'

'Another thing is the eclipse of the moon last night, especially visible in the southwest.'

'Thank you for clearing that up, Meyer. You've restored my faith in my vision.' Their conversations are often tests of wit, paradox, and allusion. Illusion, he thinks.

Meyer says, 'How about the vision of the rightness of your move out there?'

Ethan remembers the party, the debacle of decking his boss. 'It was right. It is, absolutely. As a matter of fact, Meyer, I have to get ready for an appointment with my boss. I promise to call soon.' He puts the phone down thinking my dear, feared, famous father.

***

This phone call is Meyer's first entry into the novel. It's self-centred to the point of rudeness; the narrator states that it's typical. Ethan's response is also understood as typical. His first words are a polite 'Good morning, Meyer', and he never finds the courage to tell his father what he thinks. To Meyer's question 'Why didn't you call?' he only *thinks* 'Because of this... because you haven't said hello or asked how I am...' Further along in the book, there are flashback scenes in Boston which show Ethan's acceptance of, even deference to, his father's selfishness as if it were a sign of real affection. What I, as writer, wanted here was the beginning of a more objective view simply because there are so many miles between them.

The subject of this call begins Meyer's characterization. He's attempting nothing less than to control his image from beyond the grave, and Ethan's ironic intervention – 'Will I be among the invited?' – is immediately squashed by Meyer's 'Who do you imagine will send the invitations?' It's witty, but dismissive: it will be Ethan's task to organize the funeral exactly as Meyer directs.

When I wrote Meyer's 'How about your vision of the rightness of your move out there?' I intended it as a continuation of his barely disguised bullying, but seeing it on the page, I understood that Meyer's nearly solipsistic egotism could also make him – supposed brilliant thinker – a stupid man. Ethan has only been away from Boston for 24 hours, no time to reflect on whether the move was right for him or not. But Meyer can't see this.

Thinking of the implications of dialogue early in the writing helped me to understand what Meyer might be capable or incapable of doing as the novel developed.

The next phone call occurs in a flashback which traces the origins of Meyer's thoughts about his own funeral. This occurs when Ethan has begun his affair with the graduate student, Sandy, at the small university in Boston where Ethan was working.

**

Meyer had made that clear the first time he spoke of his funeral, the day after Ethan introduced him to Sandy. Meyer phoned him at his Thoreau office and said, 'It's Dad. Are you busy?'

'Dad' was no good omen; he never called himself Dad.

Ethan said, 'I'm marking student papers, grateful for the interruption.'

There was a silence, but silence was a feature of their talk.

Ethan said, 'What did you think of Sandy?'

Meyer said, 'As I said last night, I think she's very nice.'

There was another silence.

Ethan said, '"Very nice" is what you say when the Bruins score out of a power play.'

'Are you fond of this girl?' Meyer asked.

'Head over heels fond. Tell me what you think of her.'

Ethan was neither angered nor abashed by the ensuing silence. He was used to Meyer thinking carefully before he spoke. It was Meyer who had told Ethan the joke: Two philosophers meet in a corridor of the university. One says, 'Good morning.' The other says, 'Define your terms.' Sometimes these defining silences of Meyer would last for months. Then he'd say, as if out of the blue, 'I've been thinking of what you said…' This silence was shorter than months. It was forty seconds long. Ethan knew it without looking at his watch, so practiced was he in this speech gap assessment.

Meyer said, 'First impressions, by definition. A sensitive, intelligent girl. A sweet smile, for sure. And a knockout figure, to these old widower's eyes. Also, it's obvious she's very taken with you.'

'So you like her.'

'Yes. She was reserved, as was I, under the circumstances of a first meeting. I believe I'll like her even more, as I get to know her better.'

Ethan said, 'But? There's a "but" in there bursting to get out.'

The silence now, though not so long, was intense.

'Since you ask,' said Meyer, 'I cannot in the long run see you being happy with a twenty-one year old. You'll say eleven years is no big difference. That was sometimes the case when I was your age, but these days, each decade is a cultural generation with a different world view. Put another way, the teacher-pupil relationship is fine – for teachers and pupils. For life partners, it's intolerable. I know how intense you are, Ethan, how much you want. The girl will tire of you as her teacher and you'll get hurt.'

'I'm more Sandy's student than she's mine.'

'Very gallant, and, I have no doubt, true, in this head-over-heels phase of the relationship. Besides, there's the ethnic business to consider.'

'Ethnic business? Last night you seemed to find her thesis on the American-Croat experience fascinating.'

'Well, yes, as cultural idea. But this deconstructing American politics to find European patterns worries me on the personal level.'

'Meaning?'

'My father didn't flee the Old World so that his grandson would spiritually re-emigrate.'

This silence, Ethan's, did not have a cognitive cause. He was just speechless. Then he said, 'Meyer, that's preposterous. If one of my grandfather's reasons for coming to America was to found a make-believe Yankee dynasty, that was his problem, not mine. Frankly, I'm shocked. I didn't expect neo-con xenophobia from you.'

Meyer said, 'Nor did you get it. My beloved Marion and I named you Ethan because it's an Old Testament *and* a New England name. I had you circumcised *and* I took you to Brooks Brothers for your first suit.'

'Yes, and that was *your* social experiment. What I know is that I love Sandy. She makes me happy. Happy. I hope that's all right, inasmuch as the perfect ethnic and generational-compatible XHelen made me miserable. Do you, at least in theory, approve of my being happy, for a change?'

Myer's voice softened. 'Of course I do. I'm only thinking of your happiness. I apologize for offending you.'

'Me, too. I shouldn't have raised my voice.'

An understandable silence occurred.

Meyer said, 'Ethan, Sandy is a fine young woman, and I'm sure I'll be very fond of her. Are you thinking of children?'

'Not thinking of it. Thinking no of it.'

After a pregnant silence, Meyer said, 'Ah.'

Ethan, trying to lighten the mood, said, 'Sandy's a Pirates fan and doesn't like the Yankees. I think we could turn her on to the Red Sox as her American League favorite.'

Meyer said, 'Yes, we'll all go to the ballgame. Ethan, I want to ask you something. What would you say my best work was?'

'Besides what you're working on now? I'd say The Ambiguity of Opposites.'

'I was afraid you'd say that.'

'Why afraid?'

'Because I wrote it so long ago and it's so popular – for philosophy, that is – and because it fixes me so narrowly.'

'It's not just popular. That's the one Quine raved about.'

'Yes, Willard was generous about it. But, you know, I'm almost seventy-eight. Your kindness about current work notwithstanding, I'm not… Well, we all know one's best work is done before thirty, in philosophy, or fiction, or physics.'

Ethan looked away from the receiver. How could his father say this to him, thirty-one with writer's block?

Meyer said, 'The point is, I'm thinking of how I'll be assessed at my funeral.'

***

The conversation continues. Ethan questions his father about his health but is told that he's fine. Ethan remembers this conversation because he's learned from an old family friend, Meyer's doctor, that Meyer has a deteriorating condition in his upper vertebrae which can restrict blood circulation to the brain and produce symptoms of dementia.

It was at this point in the writing that I saw it would be possible to present Meyer in the present tense of the novel solely through telephone calls and answerphone messages. I knew I wanted to do this, but I wasn't certain why, except that the idea of a disembodied voice seemed symbolic of Meyer's relationship with Ethan.

Moreover, I saw that, in the flashback, Ethan was capable of expressing reactive anger to his father, though quickly ashamed of doing it. This gave me the idea that Ethan was trying to defend his ideal image of both his father's and his own rational, 'philosophical' stance. While it was clear this stance wasn't consistent with Meyer's behaviour over the telephone, it began to offer me an understanding of how Ethan's ability to believe in the soundness of his relation with his father could, indeed, had to, change during the novel. Such change couldn't be easy, and this character struggle would be an important plot mechanism. I didn't think of it in such neat novelistic terms at the time. But, looking back, I see that this is how listening to your own characters' dialogue – to what they say – is of great practical importance in figuring out your storyline.

Knowing of his father's illness but warned by the doctor to give Meyer some time to raise the topic himself, Ethan decides to make an 'ordinary' friendly phone call. Since it's a day when Meyer is at his university, Ethan calls his office and learns from his assistant that Professor Baum is on holiday in the Caribbean. Ethan's response, I now saw, had to be a struggle between his pity and a feeling of abandonment by Meyer, as if proving that his only child means less to him than having a piña colada on a palm-fringed beach.

I think it was at this point that I noticed Ethan was doing the very thing he disliked in his father – putting himself first. Seeing this gave me another insight into Ethan's character that would be important to the novel's development.

Meyer's next telephone appearance, a few weeks later, begins with answer phone messages.

***

…Back at his apartment, Ethan listens to the phone messages.
'Ethan, hello. This is Meyer. I'm back. Please call. Bye.'
'Meyer again. Give me a call, please.'
'Ethan, this is your father. I know it's early out there; two hours difference, is it? Are you asleep? I'd like to talk to you.'

Just as the message ends, the phone rings. 'Ethan?'

'Meyer, hi. How are you?'

'Better for hearing your voice, son. I miss you. I was in St. Lucia, vacationing. I fell in with a – you'll be interested to hear – a herd of Derek Walcott worshippers. Women, mostly, all of them white. By day two, I was convinced he'd fucked them all.'

'Jesus!' says Ethan, despite himself. He has never before heard Meyer say anything stronger than 'damn.'

'By day three, or was it still day two, who knows – it was a terrible time – I was convinced the sexuality was all fabulous, mass literary hallucination. I missed you. I went away to think because I learned I was ill. I know Haskell Perlmutter spoke with you. Ankylosis spondylitis. Not a Greek tennis player, a disease, as you know. Though a disease that mimics entropy. Entropy, as I see it, was Newton's most philosophically challenging discovery. Imagine, Ethan, this genius dedicated to perpetual motion, to the alchemist's dream of the philosopher's stone, the – if you will – nuclear fusion of his day, and he comes across the fact that the great clockmaker's clock is invariably winding down; the rub, as the man says. But being Isaac Newton, he investigates and *publishes* the rub. There's the rub. There is a great philosophical tract to write about entropy. The latest biographical scholarship, I believe, has it that Newton, qua man, was one of the nastiest pieces of work ever to crawl on the planet. Nevertheless, this profoundly religious and paranoid alchemist does not suppress the entropy that flesh is heir to. Spirit, also, one might say.'

His father is raving. He needs loving, calming words. Ethan can only say, 'You went down to the islands on your own, to think.'

'No, with a friend, a woman. Her name is Hannah Miller. She's forty years old and I have been seeing her for some time. However, things did not go well for us on St. Lucia. All my fault. And, at her insistence, the relationship is over, terminé, finite, kaput. She is, of all things, an anal architect, I mean a naval architect.'

'Meyer, come visit me in Albuquerque. Visit Lucy and me. She told me you've been speaking on the phone, so you'll know what's been happening to me, bad news and good. Lucy thinks you're terrific. And you should come because I miss you and love you.'

'Yes, I see. Thank you.'

There is a strange noise on the line. It takes Ethan some time to understand that this sound, like the grating of rocks, is his father crying. When he stops, they talk more of his visiting Albuquerque. He'll try to come out by Labor Day, for a week or so.

After the call, Ethan looks around the apartment wondering if it will do for Meyer. He feels he's, once again, measuring himself by his father. The shock of Meyer's eventual death, he sees, will be in catching himself continuing to perform for his father's absent applause. As a sensational non sequitur, Ethan becomes certain that his father had been unfaithful to his mother. ... Why doesn't this cause him more discomfort? Is his memory of Marion so dim? Or has he always suspected yet forgiven Meyer's infidelities out of a secret, rogue affinity? He really doesn't want to think of this...

***

Here, despite Meyer's opening protestations of being better for hearing Ethan's voice, Meyer immediately launches into a soliloquy of self-pity and a fantasy of sexual jealousy. Ethan believes he's never heard such crude language from Meyer. True, Meyer breaks down crying, but Ethan seems to put it down to his father's illness, his understanding that Meyer's dissertation on entropy was really about Meyer's struggle to face his illness, his mortality. From Ethan's point of view, it's a non sequitur that he 'suddenly' knows Meyer was unfaithful to Marion. (In an earlier flashback, Meyer has told him that not only was Marion his one and only, but that for the past 15 years since her death he's been celibate.) Once more, at this physical distance from his father, Ethan continues having more intimations of what at heart he's always known, but suppressed.

It was with the book's next telephone conversation, around a third of the way through, that I more fully understood *why* I didn't want Meyer to appear in person in the present-tense scenes.

Ethan is just about to set off on his first research trip to various sites around New Mexico for a job he's landed – writing the text for a book of photographs of environmentally sensitive places in the state. This gets him recalling that Meyer had given up driving several years before. He wonders if his father had forebodings of his illness then.

***

Touched, he phones Meyer again, wanting to talk about the drives they can take together when he visits. Ethan automatically begins with 'How are you?' Meyer replies: 'Who am I would be more appropriate, don't you think, Ethan?'
'No.'
'Haven't you believed all these years I was wholly thought, a holy thinker, in fact, a superannuated Søren Kierkegaard? And now you see me revealed as an innumerate Bertie Russell, dick-brained, sniffer of undergraduate underpants, the old dog, eh? The connoisseur of cooze?'
'Stop this, Meyer.'

'No? Then you have been very wrong, sadly misguided by me. Once, years ago, I went to your upstairs bedroom in Somerville and opened the door on Helen stepping from the shower naked. I left at once, apologizing. But for months, afterwards –'

'Don't, Meyer.'

'– years, perhaps, I masturbated thinking of her skimpy tits and slick black pubic hair. I can imagine them to this day, this minute.'

'It's the spondylitis.'

'It is not! Or if so, it is *in* spondylitis *veritas*. If I am sick, I am sick of pretending. That is my fear and trembling, and not my sickness unto death, to paraphrase your great Dane.'

'Not mine. I never much liked Kierkegaard.'

'Is that so? I thought there was an aesthetic affinity. Didn't you direct me to the early expressionist writers as a way of understanding Kierkegaard in his *Zeitgeist*? Read Georg Büchner, you said.'

'That wasn't me. Perhaps it was one of your grad students.'

'Perhaps. You don't have to have my particular condition to lose your memory. So where was I? Yes, discussing how many graduate students I've slept with.'

'Father!'

'No, Bertie Russell the fucker at least gave his wives an honest, if hard, time. I am in no way trying to be funny.'

Ethan takes a deep breath and says, 'Is it that you feel guilty about Marion?'

'Of course I do. But then, I felt guilty while Marion was alive, yet that didn't keep me from screwing around left, right, and center. Do you mind me saying all this?'

Ethan really doesn't know whether to say yes or no. He says, weakly. 'Meyer, I'm really looking forward to you being out here. There are wonderful places to go. I hear the Acoma Pueblo is spectacular.'

'And there'll be Lucy. Isn't she too old for you?'

'We'll have a nice time. The three of us will see the sights.'

'Her writing is elegant and depressing. Do you trust me not to make a pass at her?'

Ethan stays silent.

'Of course, of course. You were faithful to Helen.'

'There was a stewardess, you might remember.'

'I once knew a stewardess. A beautiful young woman, wonderful complexion, green eyes, drrrop-dead beautiful! I cannot remember her name. A fine fuck. An Irish girl.'

Ethan can't stand any more of this. 'Meyer, I need to get off the phone, to prepare for some trips.'
'But are we going to be travelling together?'
'When you're here. This is for my work, a commissioned book on New Mexico.'

**

It was this telephone conversation in which Ethan hears from his father's mouth the confirmation of Meyer's infidelity to his mother that he felt certain of even before the call, which made clear to me the idea that the most important reason for keeping Meyer physically separated from Ethan in the present tense of the book was that Meyer should be presented in this way as the voice in Ethan's mind. From then on in the writing, I knew that the main psychological tension in the novel was within himself, between Ethan and that part of him I could think of as Meyer-in-Ethan. This also made clear to me that doing this would entail crossing the boundaries of dominance between the competing characteristics.

As a result of this thinking, the night before Ethan sets out on his car trip, the following takes place:

…The phone wakes him. It's still dark. He puts the phone to his ear and hears. 'Remember that I do not like William James.'

Ethan is so disoriented, he assumes he's fallen asleep in the middle of a conversation. He says, 'The American Bentham.'
'Good, you remember. From utilitarianism to pragmatism is nothing but the loss of ethics.'

Ethan rubs his eyes. 'Maybe Unitarianism was also a version of utilitarianism. The words –'

'Oh, no, no, no,' says Meyer. 'Puns are no substitute for scholarship. I abjure Derrida and his leaden, linguistic play. Bentham, at any rate, begins from ethics, though he's not much, philosophically. He was essentially a political and social reformer. Oh, my, I'm giving you an old undergraduate lecture, "Adam Smith and the Ethics of Self-Interest." Well, Ethan, this is the dying mind. It's terrible. Terrifying. What time is it?'

Ethan, terrified for and by his father, says, 'Philosophy is the last all-male club. You're a philosopher for the same reason you're a philanderer.' Does he mean a wanderer, a meanderer?

Meyer says, 'What are you going on about?'

Ethan says, 'I know I'm responsible for everything I've done, yet I see you were my model. Model, mode, my way.'
'Please stop derridaing me, I mean deriding me. Now you have me doing it.'

Ethan is emboldened by sleepiness. 'Of course you want to play. But as you grow older it becomes more difficult to separate the philanderer from the philosopher; his hand is in your pocket. But why me, Meyer? What so excites you about my women – projected incest?'

'Ha! You don't remember your mother, how she was with you?' The Yiddish syntax and inflection are rare for Meyer.

'How was she?'

'Marion never abused you, of course. But such smoochie-coochie smother love!'

'You were jealous.'

'If anything, this aroused me for her, this carrying on with you so openly. Perhaps it might be that her total openness in loving you is what I yearned for but couldn't give. Remember, the ethical problem for philosophy is not how people should behave, but how *thinking* people should behave.'

This seems such an indictment of thinking people that it shocks Ethan awake. He says, 'I don't understand.'

Meyer says, 'No wonder. Here's my watch and it says a quarter past four. Another time, please call earlier. Or later. Good night.'

'Good night, Meyer.' Ethan puts down the phone knowing he'll wake up unsure of who called whom or even if there was a call.

Next morning, no sooner does Ethan drive past the city limits than he decides to call his father from a gas station phone booth.

...He ducks and crouches under the plastic dome and calls.

'Meyer Baum,' his father says loudly, so that it sounds like Meyer Bomb.

Ethan takes one from his father's book and starts with: 'What you said about pragmatism.'

'Ethan, is that you?'

'It seems, on reflection, bass-ackwards. Dewey and James made a profoundly radical critique of conventional philosophy – that all of its standards followed from living, and –'

'Where are you? I hear traffic noise.'

'– and that philosophers therefore could not remove themselves from life, as they pretended to. This was an impossible position – logically, ethically, or aesthetically.'

'Ah, yes, you're out there in the brave new west, but there is history, even intellectual history, despite that.'

'Meyer, do you really not believe that our lives justify our thoughts?'

'There is something far too a priori in that formulation. Have you been reading Richard Rorty? Rorty's a nice enough fellow, but though he uses philosophical methodology, he's not much more than a sensualist.'

'No, I haven't been reading Rorty. And, yes, I believe that life itself is the inevitable, the grand a priori.'

'Very clever. But that's a writer's cleverness, and that's why Rorty is only a Whitmanesque commentator. Ethan, where are you?'

Ethan unwinds from the booth to look. Some cars and a pickup truck come over the crest of the road. Way up behind is the mountain Lucy almost dropped from. He turns: down the bare slope between the buildings is a long chain link run. There are wolves there. Of course not. They're German shepherds. He says, 'At a kennels, Meyer, in Cedar Crest, just outside Albuquerque.'

'Are you buying a dog?'

'No, I'm… Maybe. I'm just looking. I'm on the start of a day trip.'

'I see. The dog would protect you.'

Ethan sees a very small boy walking down the slope towards the dog-run. 'Protect me from what? All the German shepherds, I mean wolves, were killed a long time ago down here.' As the boy nears the fence, three dogs rush at him, barking. They leap at the fence and stay reared against it, twice the boy's height, barking madly, nipping at each other with teeth Ethan can see gleaming even from this distance. The boy goes right up to the fence and the dogs come down, muzzles at the chain link. The boy puts in his hand. Ethan waits for the scream, but the dogs are licking him, tongues through the fence, knocking each other sideways in a frenzy of affection for the small, grabbing hand. The boy is laughing and shouting at them.

'Ethan?'

'I'm here.' A woman's voice calls, 'Billy, Billy, Billeeee! Didn't I say no? Get up out of there, Billy!' The woman walks down the slope into the wind. Her long, pale dress blows back tight against her pregnant belly and breasts. Ethan wishes he were the husband watching from the house, wanting her to finish dealing with Billy so that he, wild about her pregnant, can be with her again. Ethan says, 'I'm here, Meyer, philosophizing. Why, really, have you been calling Lucy?

'To get to know her. Can you be jealous?'

'Yes. Why not?'

'It's true, she's attractive, a fine figure.'

'How do you know that?'

'The book jackets. Besides, I asked her to send me a photo. It was here when I returned. Didn't she tell you about the photo? It doesn't matter. It means nothing to her.'

Ethan doesn't like Lucy not telling him. He doesn't like his father telling him. Down by the dog-run, the woman has picked up the boy and holds him with one arm, at her hip. The boy's face is on her stomach, as if listening. She's walking up the slope, smiling.

'Meyer, what is it with you and women?'

'I like them. I feel comfortable and comforted. You know, you didn't get all your good looks from your mother. I'll give you a bit of advice, if I may, which I never did when you were with Helen.'

'Not so,' Ethan says, bitterly. 'You were forever advising me in your ostensibly rational way, when it turns out you were masturbating to your memory of her naked in the shower. Good lord.'

'Here's the advice: if Lucy should happen to enjoy a little flirting with me, allow it. Tolerate it. Enjoy it.'

'At least you've dropped the veneer of rationality. What a gem of self-interested advice. Meyer, Lucy is too old for you, and, please understand, if I ever catch you touching her, I'll bite off your hand.'

Meyer laughs: 'What, the hand that fed you? Ethan, I am an old man. A bona fide geezer. Have no fear.'

'I have to get back to the road now.' Ethan is ashamed of the entire conversation.

'Right. Call again, soon. This has been one of our best phone calls ever: philosophy, dogs, women. Terrific! Lots of love, son.'

Ethan hangs up. His hand is stiff from squeezing the receiver.

***

It's little wonder Meyer so enjoys the conversation. He could be talking to himself, so much has Ethan 'come out' of the Meyer closet. Even his ironic 'I'm here, Meyer, philosophizing', spoken as he fantasizes about the attractive pregnant woman he's watching, is as much a homage to Meyer as it is a critique. Yet at the end if the call, Ethan, is still swinging back to being 'ashamed of the entire conversation'.

Meyer's next call to Ethan, several days later, is made in a less ebullient, more confrontational mood. He informs Ethan that he keeps a quote from Cicero in his working desk: '*Nihil tam absurde dici potest, quod non dicatur ab aliquo philosophorum.*' Meyer says, 'It means: Nothing so absurd can be said that hasn't already been said by a philosopher.' He goes on to admit that Ethan's point about mainstream philosophy being out of touch with real life is true. He has to have rational moments. As the writer, I have to maintain the credibility of the entire character, not only of the character at his extremes. Meyer could not have so deep an effect on Ethan if, besides his charm and outrageous behaviour (and remember that dialogue *is* behaviour), he wasn't capable of seeing and admitting to character flaws and wrong he's done. Though not to all of them – he never owns up to the poison dart of his innocent-seeming question about Lucy sending him a photo of herself: 'Didn't she tell you about the photo?'

In this conversation, Meyer asks politely if Lucy and Ethan might want to have a child. And he's able to add, 'To have a grandchild would give me such, would be such – a blessing.' The stops and starts in the phrasing signal how difficult it is for Meyer to reach beneath verbal brilliance to emotional truth. His ability to do so late in life, and when ill, works to keep the father–son relationship passionately complex.

Other calls from Meyer are presented in another telephone format. One is to put off his visit to Albuquerque because he's finally started work on an idea he's had years before. Ethan, for a number of reasons, replies (in another call) that it would even be better postponed to late September, since the weather wouldn't be so burning hot then. It's to turn out that Meyer has 'started work' with a 24-year-old woman. I have Meyer present his excuse in one of two long answerphone messages he leaves for Ethan. Having Meyer speak in monologue allows the reader to hear the uninterrupted, perfectly rational voice that can fool everyone.

Another telephone variation is a conversation between Meyer and Lucy overheard by Ethan, when he picks up an extension in Lucy's house just as the other two start speaking. (At this point, Lucy's daughter Emmy is very ill.)

…Ethan picks up the phone just after Lucy does, hears his father's voice, and listens.

'Lucy, dear, how's Emmy? How are you?'

'She's a little better, improving. I'm okay. How are you?'

'Fine. Is Emmy still in critical condition?'

'Yes, but they hope to be upgrading her to "serious" today or tomorrow. She recognized me and Ethan. She says hi.'

'Oh, Lucy. Poor you. This is something only a parent can understand.'

'Meyer, Ethan has been wonderful.'

'Of course. He's such… I was imagining how I would have felt had Ethan as a teenager gone through something like this. I can tell you, I wept just to imagine it.'

'Oh, Meyer.'

'I'm sorry I'm not there to do whatever, to share the hard times. Especially as it might help make up for certain times I feel I let Ethan down.'

'Thank you. No one could be more supportive than Ethan. You can be proud of him.'

'Of course, Lucy. I understand why this wouldn't be a good time for me to be there, not that I'd need any looking after, for heaven's sake; I've looked after myself for seventy-eight years now. No, something about me irritates Ethan, always has.'

'Meyer, he's trying to pull himself up from a low point in his writing, and, well, there you are a famous philosopher. It's a difficult situation. Anyway, we both hope you'll be out here as soon as Emmy's better.'

'That's good of you, Lucy. You're able to say things that, frankly, Ethan never can with me. I feel close to you, dear, even over the phone. I know you're good for Ethan. And you know I wish what you do for your dear daughter.'

'That's kind of you. Would you like to speak to Ethan?'

'No, no. That's all right. Give him my love.'

'And ours to you, Meyer.'

Ethan quietly puts the phone down.

As the readers 'hear' this conversation, they know Ethan is overhearing it, and I hope they imagine some of the conflicting feelings going through his mind. Meyer can be heard as being completely sincere or as playing a game of cat and mouse. Saying things to exclude Ethan from the shared misery only parents can know. But, at Lucy's slightest protestation of Ethan's wonderful behaviour, Meyer immediately turns it to a statement of his own failure at deep communication with Ethan, or about a certain wariness on the part of his beloved son. So Ethan can be touched by Meyer and jealously angered at the same time. He has to keep quiet, but he has to hear this out.

The final reference to Meyer's telephone calls in the novel's present tense presents still another variation of telephone formatting. As Ethan is about to leave on a later research trip for the book he's writing, Lucy says, 'Say something to make me feel happy.'

… 'I'm feeling good about the inanity of Meyer's calls. His "Ethan, I'm so happy with Yang [his young girlfriend]." Or, "Hello, Ethan. You have no idea how happy I am with Yang. I had no idea I could be so happy." Yesterday I called him, determined to have a more adult conversation content. Yang Chou answered, and I found myself saying, "I have to tell you, you make my father very happy." And what I got for this was Yang saying, "Meyer makes me very happy. I can't believe how happy he makes me." And rather than making me feel slightly sick, all this made me feel happy.'

Hearing this all in Ethan's voice shifts its meaning to his attempt to respond to Lucy's request. It's a poor response: it substitutes 'happy' for what he knows she really wants to hear that he loves her. A secondary purpose is to relate at speed what would at this point in the novel be too slow a presentation, call by call.

This Case study demonstrates how character can be presented in a secondary format, and how such a presentation can influence the plot and even suggest thematic development that might not have surfaced if presented 'in person', rather than in this complex, suggestive telephone voice.

Character, plot and theme can be developed through a dialogue format different from direct dialogue but running parallel to it in the novel or short story. The secondary format can add variety and special focus to the writing.

How vividly individualized can other 'dialogue' formats be?

This question puts 'dialogue' in quotation to indicate a questionable use of the term. For those of us old enough to have been letter writers, the electronic substitutes seem on the whole lacking in character – that is, lacking in individuated voice. The fascinating letter writer has become merely the informative emailer; the emailer becomes the blandly utilitarian text message writer or the twit tweeter. Much social messaging is personal advertising or little more than a shorthand of no real character.

Put another way, writing realistic dialogue or character in 'voice' in these formats is not realistic, since it occurs so rarely out there in reality.

Yet you may know some one or two whose emails are as vivid and individual as good letter writing or good speech. Moreover, you're writing fiction, so why not try to sometimes get some character into what in real life is generally so lacking in character or individual voice.

It's important to remember that this does not mean that the authorial control of these ordinary IT formats can't be dramatic. Even a one-word message, perfectly timed (perfectly placed) can really move the story along or change its direction. The point is that by their highly practical, time-saving nature, these are more naturally devices of narrative than of dialogue. Nevertheless, as I, you have probably read some short fiction entirely composed of exchanges in IT format. (These are not the same as fictional creations of 'new' languages in an all IT future, whether in science fiction or fantasy genres.)

Write

Write a three-page 'dialogue' in a fairly realistic IT format – email, text message or social network. Then see if it a) reads believably, b) sounds like dialogue. Finally, revise it so that one of the characters communicating this way is able to present a memorable 'voice' in this format.

Focus points

Chapter 5 has looked at a range of major formats different from ordinary direct dialogue in which to present dialogue. Its main ideas are summarized in the following five points:

- Letters, being written communication, can present within them ordinary direct dialogue. While formal letter writing doesn't intend to present the speech representation of the writer, informal letter writing certainly may.

- The time lag between letters in a correspondence makes it different from two or more characters speaking face to face. This can provide the opportunity for plot mechanisms like wrong assumptions and misinterpretations useful for the writer.

- Journals and diaries offer further possibilities for the use of the character's voice. Since a common distinction between the two formats is that diaries are generally held to be private writing, intended for the author's eyes only, their discovery by other characters can provide significant plot and relationship developments. The journal is often used for a more thoughtful, reflective interpretation of the events and characters. With letters, both of these formats can provide a range of voices in a fully or partly historical piece of fiction.

- Telephone conversations are pure dialogue, with participants physically separated. When the format is answerphone or voicemail, it is like short monologue but also like letters with a potentially very short time gap. Telephone conversations and messages can be reported by one character to another; depending on memory and point of view, this can represent the original voice on a scale of exact accuracy to complete reinvention by the speaker. The variety of telephone formats can produce complex character development and relationships, as well as insights for the writer as to where to go next with character, plot and even theme.

- While emails and other electronic (IT) formats are not in real life generally vehicles that present individuated voices, there's nothing stopping the writer from trying to give them more dialogue-like characteristics.

Chapter 6 looks at the uses of direct dialogue and of indirect speech. It also focuses on how to make transitions in and out of dialogue effectively coherent.

6

Direct and indirect speech and transitions

In this chapter you will learn:

- What indirect speech is and how it differs from direct speech
- How to use indirect speech in your writing
- What is meant by transitions into and out of direct and indirect speech
- How transitions can create a range of effects that develop scenes and characters.

Direct speech (dialogue or direct quotation) is easy enough to define: it's the representation in writing of a person or persons speaking. It's simply characters' speech.

Indirect speech, or indirect quotation, is more complex. It's not necessarily what someone has actually said but what the narrator and/or character says has been said.

Imagine a scene between Margaret Pickering and her 14-year-old son David. Margaret's 12-year-old daughter Rosemary is not present. The scene takes place on a Wednesday.

> David put his empty milk glass on the counter. 'Mom, can Rosie and me go to the carnival on Saturday?'
>
> 'This Saturday,' she said, and paused to think.
>
> David didn't like it when she paused to think. It usually meant no.
>
> She said, 'How much longer does the carnival run?'
>
> He said, 'It closes at the end of the weekend after this.'
>
> 'All right, here's what we'll do. This Saturday you'll both help clean the garden, as you promised. And then you can go next Saturday. Okay?'
>
> 'Okay.'
>
> 'But before you do, both of you have to tidy your rooms. They are now beyond impossible.'
>
> 'Mom, my room's excellent.'
>
> 'Excellent?'
>
> David smiled. 'Excellent for me.'
>
> 'I can hardly move in there, let alone vacuum. And you've been promising to clean it for over a month.'
>
> 'Oh, Mom.'
>
> 'No "oh, Mom" about it. You both do your rooms or you won't go. And tell your sister.'
>
> 'Okay, I'll tell her. I promise.'
>
> 'And you can start by rinsing your milk glass and putting it in the dishwasher.'
>
> 'Yes, Mom. I'm doing it. See?'

Now, two days later on Friday, imagine the following scene between David and his sister Rosemary (Rosie).

> 'So did you ask Mom?'
>
> David didn't look up from the display screen in his hand. 'About what?'

'You know, about the carnival tomorrow.'

'Yeah, it's okay. We can go.'

Rosie frowned. 'She actually said that?'

'Yeah,' David said, 'she said that we could go on Saturday. But we have to clean up our rooms.'

Here, you could assume selective memory on David's part. He has forgotten about cleaning up the garden; this also involves forgetting that tomorrow is not the Saturday that they can go. But note that David hasn't *said* anything which is untrue. His mother did say they could go on Saturday, and she did say they had to clean up their rooms. David might insist on this in the argument with his mother and Rosie that would probably arise later in the day or next morning.

A different characterization and sibling relationship could produce different indirect dialogue, as in the following scene, on the same Friday:

Rosie said, 'I'll bet you didn't speak to Mom, did you?'

'I did.' David didn't look up from his war game.

'Well, what did she say?'

'About what?'

'About tomorrow. The carnival? Duh!'

'She said you couldn't go.' He spoke to the small screen between his hands. 'She said that you had to clean up the garden and something else... Yeah, you had to clean up your room. She said it was a shithole.'

'She did not. That's gross. You're such a liar!'

'Only kidding. She said your room was impossible. Believe me. Or don't. I don't care.

Rosie bit at her thumbnail. Then she said, 'So what did she say about you and your room?'

'That's my business.'

'You're mean. Do you know that?'

'Hey, why don't you get off your butt and ask her yourself?' he said, continuing to play.

Rosie said, 'You're mean and you're a geek.'

Here, David maliciously fails to mention himself. Again, what he's said is true, but knowingly incomplete.

The scene could be presented mainly in narrative, this time with Rosie providing the aggravation:

David was sitting in the kitchen playing Kombat Kommando Killers when Rosie came in.

They nodded at each other. She went to the fridge, took out the milk and poured herself a glass. She sat on the edge of the table opposite David and took a few small sips. Then she asked what their mother had said about the carnival. David paused the game and told her she'd asked how long the carnival was on for, and when he'd said until the end of the next weekend, she told him they could go on that Saturday but tomorrow they had to help clean up the garden, and also she said they had to clean up their rooms before they could go.

Rosie said, 'That's so unfair. Are you sure that's what she said?'

When David said he was, Rosie said that it just had to be tomorrow because next Saturday was Susie's birthday party and she wasn't going to miss that and she really, really wanted to go to the carnival. David said she should go and ask their mom about it. Rosie said no she wouldn't because what was the use once Mom made up her mind, and it was rotten because she was old enough to go out on her own and didn't need David to take her everywhere and that this just ruined everything.

You notice that the scene above has two types of indirect speech. One is David's fairly factual summary of their mother's injunctions and requirements before they can go. The other is the indirect speech given Rosie in the final paragraph. This slips closer to Rosie's way of speaking with the repetition of 'really' and the long last sentence which imitates the rhythm of a speaking voice, though keeping it indirect because of the use of 'she' rather than 'I'.

The initial scene between David and his mother might not be presented in the writing. It might be more dramatic to have it referred to in the argument that occurs, say, on the Saturday morning when either or both children expect to go to the carnival. There, the implications of the 'editing' done by the character in relating the original speech become apparent.

 Key idea

Indirect speech can be used in narrative or in dialogue both to summarize what has been said by one or more people or to relate it so as to alter what has been said. The alteration may be intentional or not.

Write

Take a dialogue scene you've written for two people and have one of them report it as indirect speech to someone else. Have your character alter some of its contents to suit the relationship with this third person.

Are all reports of or references to what has been spoken considered indirect speech?

Short answer: No. Common sense should be the guide.

Following are three examples of reports of or references to what has been spoken. Which do you identify as indirect speech?

1   The commencement address had been unusually frank. Mr Berk spoke of why we should give thanks to banks, the need for greed, and how social welfare led to warfare.

2   'My mother warned me against men like you. She also warned me about wearing clean underwear in case I was knocked over by a bus.'

3   The time has come, the waitress said, to talk of many things – of choux and chips and Swedish lax, of mortgages and bling, and why the peas were spoiled rot, and whether figs have flings.

Example 1 has no indirect speech. It's simply a narrative summary of topics within a speech.

Example 2 has a first sentence which really isn't a character using indirect speech. Her mother might have warned her against all sorts of men, but it's very unlikely she said 'I warn you against men like him', since the cliché means a general warning to be on guard, etc. The second sentence, though also cliché, could be indirect speech; that is, her mother may have said, 'Always make sure you wear…' etc.

Example 3 is all direct speech, what 'the waitress said'. Remember that quotation marks are not invariably used to mark direct speech.

Is indirect speech always simple to identify?

Short answer: 'Always' isn't always a useful word in figuring out fiction.

Here's a paragraph from Angela Carter's story 'Black Venus's Tale', fiction based on a real person, Jeanne Duval, the mistress of Charles Baudelaire.

> Nadar says he saw her a year or so after, deaf, dumb and paralysed, Baudelaire died. The poet, finally, so far estranged from himself that, in the last months before the disease triumphed over him, when he was shown his reflection in a mirror, he bowed politely, as to a stranger. He told his mother to make sure that Jeanne was looked after but his mother didn't give her anything. Nadar says he saw Jeanne hobbling on crutches along the pavement to the dram-shop; her teeth were gone, she had a mammy-rag tied around her head but you could still see that her wonderful hair had fallen out. Her face would terrify the little children. He did not stop to speak to her.

(Think of the following comments as an exercise in common sense.) There are three points in this paragraph where indirect speech is signalled: at the first 'Nadar says', at 'He told' and at the second 'Nadar says'.

Remember, this is fiction, though fiction about real people and using their names. Suppose you know that Nadar was an early photographer, a close friend of Baudelaire, and that Jeanne Duval had been his mistress before being Baudelaire's. Might this change how you understand 'Nadar says'? After all, the expression 'X says' can not only mean that X speaks or spoke the words but also that X wrote the words in a letter or journal or newspaper or book.

If you didn't know who Nadar was, you might well think that the story's narrator (third person) was referring in both 'Nadar says' instances to something actually spoken by Nadar. On the other hand, if you did know about him, might you wonder if the narrator was referring to something he wrote? And would this make the more knowledgeable reader among you more confused?

Leaving the problem aside for a moment, it's clear that both the more and less knowledgeable reader would identify the clause following 'He told' as indirect speech, probably of a summarizing sort.

Returning to the problem: the answer is that the problem shouldn't exist, even if you were a scholar of the life of Nadar. This is fiction, and whether you imagine as you read that the words were spoken or written by Nadar, you should hear it in this storytelling as indirect speech. Why? Because that's the spirit of the writing, to create a sense of living people from historical personages.

So Nadar says this and that about Jeanne. So Baudelaire told his mother to do this and that for Jeanne. Common sense, yes, but also remember that what you're reading in this book is intended as common sense *for a writer*, how to grasp what you read so that you can use it for your own purposes – that sort of common sense.

Focus point

Use your common sense as a writer to make your own use of any form of direct and indirect speech you come across in your reading, hearing and imagination.

What is meant by transitions into and out of direct and indirect speech?

The basic formal elements of fiction involved in transitions are narrative, dialogue and indirect dialogue (indirect speech). The transition is simply the shift from one to another.

For the purposes of this book, a transition from dialogue to narrative is considered to be from a scene in which dialogue dominates into narrative of a substantial length – several paragraphs or more. The same would apply to a scene of sections predominantly narrative; here the shift would involve more than one or two consecutive statements of dialogue.

For transitions from narrative to indirect speech and from indirect to direct speech and vice-versa, the form shifted to need not extend so long. The point is not a mechanical definition by length of shift but, in all these instances, to recognize what the transition is achieving and how you can use such shifts in your own writing.

Case study: Richard Russo, *Empire Falls*

This involves a return to the novel cited in Chapter 1, Richard Russo's *Empire Falls*. (Note: The Prologue and chapters set in the past are presented in italics.)

Extract 1

...Whiting men had a lot in common, including the fact that they invariably married women who made their lives a misery. C. B.'s

father had fared better in this respect than most of his forebears, but still resented his wife for her low opinion of himself, of the Whiting mansion, of Empire Falls, of the entire backward state of Maine, to which she felt herself cruelly exiled from Boston.

The lovely wrought iron gates and fencing that had been brought all the way from New York to mark the perimeter of the estate were to her the walls of her prison, and every time she observed this, Honus reminded her that he held the key to those gates and would let her out at any time. If she wanted to go back to Boston so damn bad, she should just do it. He said this knowing full well she wouldn't, for it was the particular curse of the Whiting men that their wives remained loyal to them out of spite.

The obvious shift in this paragraph of narrative is into indirect speech, coming after 'Honus reminded her that he held the key to those gates and would let her out at any time.' You then hear his voice in the next statement: 'If she wanted to go back to Boston so damn bad, she should just do it.' The following statement, beginning 'He said this knowing…' shifts back from indirect dialogue to narrative. The indirect speech brings life and character into the narrative. More specifically, it dispels the possibility of stereotyping. This means that the richest man in central Maine is shown in his language – 'so damn bad' (not even 'so *damned* bad') – not to be particularly refined in speech but still close to his rural, hardworking origins.

A subtler shift occurs in the narration of Honus's resentment of his wife 'for her low opinion of himself, of the Whiting mansion, of Empire Falls, of the entire backward state of Maine…' Here, the word 'backward' is certainly the wife's word for it, Honus being very satisfied with what he makes of and from the place. This suggestion of another voice, of his wife's voice in his resentment of her, contributes a slight but real touch of both their characters. And this is particularly important in the context of the historical sweep of this prologue, where the writer's job is to give the background of the town of Empire Falls and its central characters, while interesting the readers in what they were 'actually' like as people.

In the next extract, the novel's central character, Miles Roby, is with his teenage daughter Tick, who's working in his restaurant after school. Miles and his wife Janine have separated, so he doesn't get to see as much of his daughter as before since he's moved out of the family home.

Extract 2

'I can do that,' Tick said when she saw her father start scraping dishes into the garbage and stacking them in the plastic rack for the next load.

'Never doubted it,' her father assured her. 'How was school?'

She shrugged. 'Okay.'

There was precious little Miles would have changed about his daughter, but to his way of thinking far too many things in Tick's life were 'okay.' She was a smart kid, one who knew the difference between first-rate, mediocre and piss-poor, but like most kids her age she seemed bored by such distinctions. How was the movie? Okay. How were the French? Okay. How's your sprained ankle feeling? Okay. Everything was pretty much okay, even when it wasn't; even when in fact it was piss-poor. When the entire emotional spectrum, from despair to ecstasy, could be summed up by a single four-letter word, what was a parent to do? Even more troubling was his suspicion that 'okay' was designed specifically as a conversation stopper, employed in hopes that the person who'd asked the question would simply go away.

The trick, Miles had learned, was not to go away. You didn't ask more probing questions, because they, too, would be met with this monosyllabic evasion. The trick was silence. If there was a trick.

'I made a new friend,' Tick finally elaborated once the Hobart [dishwashing machine] had shuddered to a halt and she'd raised the doors to extract the tray of clean dishes.

Miles rinsed his hands and went over to where Tick was stacking the warm plates. He took one down from the shelf and checked it, relieved to find it squeaky clean. The Hobart would live.

'Candace Burke. She's in my art class. She stole an Exacto knife today.'

'What for?'

Tick shrugged. 'I guess she didn't have one. She starts all her sentences with oh-my-God-oh-my God. Like, Oh-my-God-oh-my-God my mascara's running. Or, Oh-my-God-oh-my-God, you're even skinnier than last year.

***'

This dialogue scene contains several transitions worth mentioning. The first follows Miles's question 'How was school?' and Tick's reply 'Okay'. The shift is from direct dialogue into a paragraph (beginning 'There was precious little') of narrative representing 'his [Miles's] way of thinking' about 'okay' as a universal response to any question he asked Tick. But after two sentences of narrative (third-person omniscient, from Miles's point of view) the paragraph shifts to indirect dialogue, and you read an exchange between Miles and Tick as imagined and/or remembered by Miles. Since Miles has actually asked in dialogue how school was and Tick has actually answered in dialogue 'Okay', you can hear the extension of 'actual' dialogue in this hypothetical dialogue. It is, as a matter of fact, presented as direct dialogue without quotation marks.

The paragraph then returns to narrative, and the short following paragraph of narrative gives Miles's trick for getting more than the 'okay' response. Its first requisite 'was not to go away'; its second 'was silence'.

After this trick is explained, Tick says something that is more than the word 'okay'. She actually volunteers the information 'I made a new friend.' The accompanying narrative tells you she said this after the dishwasher stopped and she'd raised its door, but the direct speech appears first.

If you look back to her last direct speech before this, you see it's that word 'Okay'. And from there to 'I made a new friend' there is no direct dialogue. In other words, the structure of Russo's writing imitates the two requirements of 'the trick': Miles does not go away and he remains silent. And it works. She speaks.

Once Tick herself introduces a subject, she can actually answer her father's question with more than 'okay'. Tick's ensuing dialogue goes into an imitation of her new friend's speech pattern. So here, within direct dialogue, is a form of indirect dialogue which is, literally, an imitation of a third person's speech, or rather her nervous tic of language, beginning every statement with 'Oh-my-God-oh-my-God'.

This relatively short extract is a good example of the power of transitions between narrative and direct and indirect speech to create a range of effects that informs, reveals and moves the scene forward while contributing a feeling of realistic complexity. That is, silences in speech in which thought takes place, thoughts in which speech takes place, and a scene in which characters not present are not only referred to but are vividly evoked.

Key idea

Transitions between narrative, direct dialogue and indirect dialogue can create many effects which deepen and develop scenes in fiction.

Write

Take a relatively straightforward scene of dialogue from your own writing or from an exercise you've written from this book and revise it by incorporating transitions into narrative and indirect dialogue so that the scene gains in characterization and story depth.

Case study: *Empire Falls* (continued)

In a chapter narrated in omniscient third person from Tick's point of view, she reflects on the non-academic track students like her friend Candace, who are known among their peers as 'Boners'.

Extract 3

…The majority are boys, who don't at all mind being referred to as 'Boners.'

Candace herself prefers 'moron.' She confessed to Tick that it's also her mother's favorite word, one she applies to Candace on a wide variety of occasions, such as, 'What's up, Moron?' or 'You learn anything in school today, Moron?' or 'Hey, Moron, you didn't walk off with my goddamn car keys again, did you?' or 'I swear to fucking Christ, Moron, I catch you in the damn liquor cabinet again, I'm going to take you out of where you are and put you in Mount Calvary with the damn Christians, let you drink the Blood of the Lamb for a while and see how well you like that shit, and I can tell you right now you won't, so just stay *out* of my fucking vodka.' As far as Tick can tell, Candace has concluded that the word is a term of endearment applied to kids like herself who happen, everyone seems to agree, to have no future.

Still, Tick wonders if she should voice her objection to the 'moron' label before explaining why she happens to be among those thus classified…

***

This transition out of reflective narration into direct speech – that of a minor character's mother, to whom this is the only reference in the novel – gives the reader insight not only to Candace, but to other characters in the novel, adult as well as teenage, who have been brought up 'to have no future'.

The transition brings a reflective section to life with its comic, brutalizing voice.

 Focus point

Brief transitions from narrative into direct dialogue can vividly *show* what the narrative has been telling.

Case study: *Empire Falls* (continued)

A similar effect can be found in the transition from narrative to indirect dialogue. The following extract occurs during a long scene of dialogue between Miles and, as he puts it, 'his soon-to-be ex-wife', Janine. Among other subjects, they have been discussing Walt Comeau, the man for whom Janine has left Miles. The extract comes at the end of a long paragraph of narrative reflection by Miles about Walt.

Extract 4

...Most people, Miles had come to understand, went about their business logically enough if you granted them a couple fundamental assumptions. No court had ordered Walt to pay rent on Miles's house, so he wouldn't. Still, he couldn't help but feel sorry for the man whose wife he'd stolen – fair and square, Walt would consider it, the better man having won – and so, even without obligation to do so, he would continue to look for little opportunities to make it up to Miles. In fact, he seemed increasingly determined to help out in any way he could. No doubt he thought his free advice was worth thousands of dollars, yet Miles stubbornly refused to implement any of it. What could you do? Talk about leading a horse to water. No, if Miles were to die in his sleep tonight, Walt would tell every last mourner that he'd tried everything he could think of to turn the Empire Grill into a profitable enterprise. Miles was a hell of a nice guy, he would conclude, but he had no head for business. Nothing about any of this would strike the Silver Fox [Walt's self-given nickname] as outrageous.

First, notice how in the first sentence of the extract the slightly formal diction of the narration is undercut by 'a couple fundamental assumptions', in which the informal 'couple' replaces the more formal 'few' and isn't presented as 'a couple of fundamental' but as 'a couple fundamental' – colloquial rather than merely informal diction. The reflections turn ironic with: 'No doubt he thought his free advice was worth thousands of dollars, yet Miles stubbornly refused to implement any of it.' Ironic, but still in the diction of Miles's inner voice.

But from the next sentence, 'What could you do?', the diction shifts to Walt's own diction [Walt has appeared in direct dialogue earlier in the book], and the narrative shifts to Walt's indirect dialogue. What's particularly enjoyable and effective is that the reader is aware that this is Walt's voice as imagined in Miles's mind – Miles's daydream of jealous sarcasm, complete with Miles pathetically imagining his own funeral.

Focus point

Transitions out of narration enable the writer to present a range of voices in direct or indirect speech to create daydreams or other fantasies.

Case study: *Empire Falls* (continued)

In this final extract of this Case study, Max, Miles's feckless father, is cadging drinks off the local reporter, Horace, in Callahan's tavern, owned by Bea Majeski. Bea is Janine's mother, the soon-to-be ex-mother-in-law of Miles. Horace, sitting at the bar with Miles, has a fibroid cyst on his forehead. Max has just suggested that Horace should have the cyst removed.

Extract 5

Max stifled a bitter laugh. 'Why? You never looked into it?'
'Never did.'
'I sure would've,' Max said. 'That son of a bitch was growing out of the middle of my forehead, I'd have looked into it pronto.'
'I think it might be the source of my intelligence,' Horace told him, winking at Bea. 'What if I let somebody cut it off and then discovered it was responsible for all my best ideas?'

'That's something Max wouldn't have to worry about,' Bea said. 'Not having a brain.'

Max treated this insult the way he treated all insults, by pushing his glass forward for a refill. In his experience, after insulting you, people generally felt guilty. It occurred to them that maybe they were selling you short. They wondered if they could do something to make it up to you. This impulse never lasted long, though, so you had to take advantage swiftly.

Max had been offering Bea opportunities to insult him all night long, but until this very moment she'd resisted, which meant she hadn't owed him anything and his glass had remained dry. Now she had no choice but to fill it and grudgingly slide it back in front of him. This time he drained off only a third, which put him in stride with Horace, right where he wanted to be.

'You ever been to Florida?' Max asked.

'Once,' Horace admitted. 'Back when I was married.'

'Before that thing started growing out of your forehead, I bet,' Max said, abruptly scooting off his stool. 'I gotta pee.'

Bea sighed when the men's room door swung shut behind him. 'You want me to run his sorry ass?' The only reasons she hadn't eighty-sixed the old fart before now was out of affection for his son Miles, who was about the nicest, saddest man in all of Empire Falls, a man so good-natured that not even being married to her daughter, Janine, had ruined him. What Janine was thinking trading in a man like Miles for a little banty rooster like Walt Comeau defied imagination. Or at least Bea's imagination. True, Miles wasn't sexy and never had been – unless you considered kindness sexy, which Bea always had. Granted, there were men you wanted to sleep with, some men because they got you all hot and bothered, but others, like Miles, you just kind of wanted to do something nice for because they were decent and deserved it and you knew they'd be appreciative and wouldn't hold it against you for maybe not being so damn beautiful yourself. Bea had tried to explain this to her daughter once, but it had come out all wrong and Janine had misunderstood completely. 'That's mercy-fucking.' she'd said, and Bea hadn't bothered to argue because her daughter, lately, considered herself an authority on all matters sexual. In fact, she'd grown tiresome on the subject, especially since Bea was just as happy to have that part of her life safely behind her. Saying good-bye to sex was like waking up from a delirium, a tropical fever, into a world of cool, Canadian breezes. Good riddance.

Miles, though, was the sort of man you could love without completely losing your self-respect, which couldn't be said for most of them, and certainly not for Walt Comeau. 'Nah, leave him be,' Horace said.

***

You've now read the extract, but if you run your eye over it without reading it, you'll see it appears to be overwhelmingly narrative, with just a few opening statements of dialogue and another short exchange of dialogue between the long narrative paragraphs.

But the extract *does not read as narrative.* You come away feeling that, for the most part, you've been hearing characters speak.

What, in fact, you've experienced is omniscient narration slipping into character – carefully making the transition from narrative to somewhere between narrative and indirect dialogue, and from there into wholly indirect dialogue. This is most often a function of shifts in person, of presentation, level of diction and particular vocabulary.

The paragraph beginning 'Max treated this insult' occurs immediately after '"That's something Max wouldn't have to worry about," Bea said. "Not having a brain."' The paragraph's first sentence is in the voice of the omniscient narrator. The second sentence begins to move closer to Max by shifting from third to second person: 'In his experience, after insulting *you* [my emphasis].' It remains in second person until the middle of the paragraph when it shifts back to third in the retrospective statement 'Max had been offering Bea opportunities to insult him all night'. And though it's narrative, it reminds the reader of the hugely rude way Max spoke to Horace: 'That son of a bitch was growing out of the middle of *my* forehead, I'd have looked into it pronto.' And that produced Bea's insult about Max not having a brain. So the voice of Max is strongly suggested by Russo's choices of shift of person and by the explanation of the 'game' Max was playing to get a free drink, an explanation which brings to mind his grossly insensitive remark to Horace.

The second long paragraph of narration uses even more types of transition to create the feeling of character voice. First, after telling you Bea sighed, it gives you direct dialogue: 'You want me to run his sorry ass?' Next, when it shifts, next sentence, back to third person, its diction has shifted from that of the paragraph's opening narrative sentence. 'The only reason she hadn't eighty-sixed the old fart before now was out of affection for his son Miles, who was about the nicest, saddest man in all of Empire Falls, a man so good-natured that not even being married to her daughter, Janine, had ruined him.' Words and phrases like 'eighty-sixed' (to stop serving someone drink or to throw them out of the premises), 'old fart', and 'about' in 'about the nicest, saddest…' bring the language of individualized, everyday speech into narrative to shift what it sounds like. And what follows is so strongly opinionated about her daughter that it strikes you as the authentic direct, funny and ironic way Bea would put it. So the form of writing is now, mid-paragraph, fully indirect speech, whose rhythm (clauses opening one out of the other in emotive rather than logical association) and whose diction is that of direct speech.

What then follows are expressions like 'in trading in a man' and 'little banty rooster'. And when the grammar demands third person, as in 'which Bea always had', it follows 'unless you considered kindness sexy' in second person and of a highly personal nature.

The writing sticks to second person in the long following sentence about what sort of man is sexually exciting to Bea – something of an internal debate in which she comes down on the side of a less sexy man like Miles being more attractive in the long run because of being more appreciative and accepting of your (her) own flaws. Note that the climax of the paragraph is Janine's response to this view – 'That's mercy-fucking' – presented in direct dialogue. And then comes the paragraph's final section, an extended denouement at Bea's happiness in waking from the 'tropical fever' of sex into the 'cool, Canadian breezes' of celibacy.

Note also that the extract ends with direct dialogue, Horace's 'Nah, leave him be', which is his response to Bea's question 'You want me to run his sorry ass?' way back at the start of the paragraph. It's clearly taken a lot longer to read the intervening writing between question and answer on the page than it would in the 'real' time of the scene. So why don't you notice and object? Because what you've read has not only been interesting, but because it's been like listening to a continuation of the *talk*, even bringing in the talk of Janine, a character who isn't there, but who contributes vividly and memorably to the 'discussion'.

It's by such use of transitions between narration, indirect and direct speech that the omniscient narrator shifts into character and can suspend the 'real' time in the scene and yet maintain the sense of realism, or at least the very willing suspension of your disbelief.

Write

Use the paragraph discussed in the above extract beginning 'Bea sighed' as a model with which to structure a paragraph about one of your own characters. This means you will be shifting from third to second person, bringing in a new character not in the scene (as Janine is brought in) and giving this character a line of direct dialogue which in one way or the other resolves the thoughts and feelings of your own character to bring the paragraph to a close.

If you're up for two exercises in one, you could lead in to your paragraph (a long one) with a question to a second character in the scene that is answered (as it is by Horace, above) after the long paragraph yet still seems to be coherent.

Focus points

Chapter 6 has focused on differences and similarities between direct and indirect dialogue and on transitions between them and narrative. Its main ideas are summarized in the following five points.

1. Indirect speech is a flexible format. It can be used in narrative as well as in direct speech. It can summarize what someone has said or be used by a character to alter what's been said either intentionally or unconsciously. At one end of a continuous scale, it can sound like narrative; at the other end like direct speech.

2. Use your common sense as a writer to make your own use of any sort of direct or indirect speech you come across in your hearing and reading.

3. Transitions between narration, indirect dialogue and direct dialogue can add multiple levels of characterization, ideas and thematic material to scenes in fiction. Transitions from narration can enable the writer to present a range of voices in direct or indirect speech in creating daydreams or other fantasies.

4 Brief transitions from narration into direct dialogue can vividly *show* what the narration has been telling. This, in turn, can fix the idea of the narrative exposition in the reader's imaginative memory by linking it to character and action.

5 Transitions from narration into direct and/or indirect dialogue can bring character(s) into narrative, contributing new material while keeping the coherence of the scene's current action.

Next step

Chapter 7 studies imitations in dialogue of multiple speech, speech in foreign languages, speech of crowds and interrupted speech.

7

Approximating the impossible: interrupted and multiple speech and the crowd scene

In this chapter you will learn:
- How to present dialogue spoken by two or more characters
- About interrupted speech
- How to manage crowd scenes
- About the different ways in which crowd dialogue can be used.

Back in Chapter 1, it was noted that it's impossible to read the dialogue of two characters speaking simultaneously. Yet people do speak at the same time. Writers have been aware of this for a long time. In Thomas Love Peacock's delightful Gothic farce *Nightmare Abbey*, published in 1818, Mr Glowry, the abbey's owner, listening at the keyhole of his son Scythrop's tower room, has distinctly heard a woman's voice inside, as well as that of his son. While pounding on the door for admittance, Mr Glowry has then heard a heavy rolling sound, as if something of massive weight were being moved. Scythrop eventually opens the door and insists there is no lady inside. He invites his father to search the room, giving him the door key to lock the exit against anyone's escape. Having invented all sorts of excuses for the 'feminine voice' his father is sure he's heard, Scythrop's one last explanation – that he's been reading out a scene from a play he's writing about The Great Mogul and his daughter Rantrorina – is the final straw for his father.

'Nonsense, sir,' interrupted Mr. Glowry. 'That is not at all like the noise I heard.'

'But, sir,' said Scythrop, 'a key-hole may be so constructed as to act like an acoustic tube, an acoustic tube, sir, will modify sound in a very remarkable manner. Consider the construction of the ear, and the nature and causes of sound. The external part of the ear is a cartilaginous funnel.'

'It won't do, Scythrop. There is a girl concealed in this tower, and find her I will. There are such things as sliding panels and secret closets.' – He sounded the room with his cane, but detected no hollowness. – 'I have heard, sir,' he continued, 'that during my absence, two years ago, you had a dumb carpenter closeted with you day after day. I did not dream that you were laying contrivances for carrying on secret intrigues. Young men will have their way; I had mine when I was a young man; but, sir, when you consider Marionetta –'

Scythrop now saw that the affair was growing serious. To have clapped his hand over his father's mouth, to have entreated him to be silent, would, in the first place, not make him so; and, in the second, would have shown a dread of being overheard by somebody.

His only recourse, therefore, was to try to drown Mr. Glowry's voice; and, having no other subject, he continued his description of the ear, raising his voice continually as Mr. Glowry raised his.

'When your cousin Marionetta,' said Mr. Glowry, 'whom you profess to love, sir –'

'The internal canal of the ear,' said Scythrop, 'is partly bony and partly cartilaginous. This internal canal is –'

'Is actually in the house, sir, and, when you are so shortly to be – as I expect –'

'Closed at the further end by the *membrana tympani* –'

'Joined together in holy matrimony –'

'Under which is carried a branch of the fifth pair of nerves –'

'I say, sir, when you are so shortly to be married to your cousin Marionetta –'

'The *cavitas tympani* –'

A loud noise was heard behind the bookcase, which...

Though writers today don't use the dashes within paragraphs as in the latter part of this extract, to separate dialogue from narrative, the conventional notation for interrupted speech remains the dash, as used by Peacock almost two hundred years ago. This also remains the convention to indicate that multiple speech is to be understood.

The other vital element of presenting dialogue as being spoken by two or more people at the same time is to actually state it to the reader, either in dialogue or, as above, in narrative: 'His only recourse, therefore, was to try to drown Mr. Glowry's voice; and, having no other subject, he continued his description of the ear, raising his voice continually as Mr. Glowry raised his.'

Mr. Glowry, of course, raises his voice in righteous indignation at his son's insistently louder evasions. So it's also the nature of the scene – the plot and character conflict – that helps the idea of the multiple dialogue seem believable.

But if, so prepared, you read the dialogue imagining it to be spoken and eventually shouted by both characters at once, you are also – because you have to – reading the dialogue in sequence; and since the scene is comic, the writer, knowing it must actually be read sequentially, can have the breaks (the interruptions) occur where the follow-ons will be oddest and funniest. So you're imagining two voices together growing in volume, but you're also reading over the dash breaks (marked /): This internal canal / Is actually in the house; when you are so shortly to be – as I expect / Closed at the further end by the *membrana tympani*/ Joined together in holy matrimony / Under which is carried a branch of the fifth pair of nerves.

If conditions are made right, as here, the writer can have it both ways at once. You're imagining a battle of multiple dialogue while at the same time enjoying the 'unintended' absurdity of the interrupted dialogue.

Key idea

The effect of multiple dialogue – two or more people speaking at once – depends on the reader being informed that it's taking place, either through narrative or dialogue, a plausible plot/character reason for its occurrence, and conventional punctuation such as the dash to indicate the switch to the other simultaneous voice. Such dialogue may also work as interrupted speech.

In the absence of any indication of multiple speech, the dash as end punctuation represents interrupted speech. Common sense suggests an interruption creates some overlap of multiple speech.

Is crowd dialogue signalled in the same way as multiple dialogue?

Voices from a crowd can be signalled by statements of narrative or dialogue, but the sense of a crowd, of the effects of its varied voices, is often implicit in character reactions.

In Ann Beattie's short story 'The Burning House', there's no direct crowd scene. There's one short dinner scene with five characters, including Sam the dog, and another short scene with three people together in the kitchen. For the rest, there are never more than two people, plus Sam, in any scene, except for several phone calls, when the voice of the caller adds another character's voice. Despite this, the feeling of the story is of a life – that of Amy, the story's narrator – being crowded into a terrible isolation. In looking at how this feeling is created, you can hopefully learn a few things about crowd scene management as a writer.

First, think of the dimensions. The story is about 6,500 words long, about 13 pages in print. Except for a flashback to a faculty lounge in the past, the story takes place on one Saturday night in Amy's house and its garden. Much of the action takes place in the kitchen and living room and voices can be heard from one to the other. The dinner scene takes place in the dining room. The final scene, at the end of the evening, takes place upstairs in the bedroom. So, physically, the story is tightly contained.

Next, characters. In addition to Amy and her husband Frank, there are four other characters who physically appear in the story: Freddy, Frank's half-brother; Tucker, an art gallery owner who employs Frank as his accountant; J.D., a friend who lives upstate but is leaving his car at Frank and Amy's and spending the night before he flies off next day; and there's Sam the dog. Amy and Frank's six-year-old son Mark is off sleeping at the house of his friend Neal and doesn't appear. Two characters appear as voices on the telephone: Marilyn, Neal's mother, and Johnny, Amy's lover.

But in addition to these eight characters, the following real and fictional characters are named in the story: Road Runner and Wile. E. Coyote (cartoon characters); James (a painter Tucker is after); James's mother; James's father; Garner (someone throwing a party that Amy attended); Natalie (Frank's lover); Larry Betwell (who told Tucker a story that Tucker is retelling); Aristotle Onassis; Stavros Niarchos; Maria Callas; J.D.'s wife and son (killed in a car crash); John Coltrane; Mark Rothko; Andrew Wyeth; Lou Reed; Frank's mother; Richard Nixon; Perry Dwyer (someone's friend); Jekyll-and-Hyde; Richard Estes, Hamlet, Nicole (Johnny's wife); and Gregor Samsa.

That's 33 named characters, counting Jekyll-and-Hyde as only one, and omitting Johnny on the telephone telling Amy he's pretending to call the National Weather Service, who says 'Hello, Weather Service', and also omitting an unnamed American artist living in France, mentioned by Tucker. And Tucker's sister is mentioned, too.

So all these characters are more present or less present in this short story in its restricted setting, in Amy's narration. And it's a present-tense narration that intensifies the onward rush of names. This rush is also intensified by Tucker's constant, ever more manic storytelling, a background torrent of namedropping. Moreover, J.D. has arrived at the dinner party late, appearing first at the kitchen window wearing a goat mask and panicking Amy who's rinsing out a glass at the sink so that she breaks it and cuts her hand. The goat man is certainly another character. And there's Freddy telling Amy about 'this man he picked up, this man who picked him up, how it feels to have forgotten somebody's name when your hand is in the back pocket of his jeans and you're not even halfway to your apartment.' This forgotten, unforgettable somebody is also squeezed into Amy's telling. Recalling another intimate scene with Freddy, she concludes, 'All those moments, and all they meant was that I was fooled into thinking I knew these people because I knew the small things, the personal things.'

Amy's son doesn't, after all, spend the night away; he's back home, sleeping. As Amy lies in bed waiting for Frank to come in from the bathroom, she hears the sounds of the house: 'water runs, the record plays, Sam is still downstairs, so there must be some action.' Then the next paragraph begins, 'I have known everybody in the house for years, and as time goes by I know them all less and less.'

Soon Frank will join her and indeed demonstrate how little she knows. You could, at this point, just about recall J.D.'s warning to Amy when she sought his advice about what she should do about herself and Johnny. 'I believe in all that wicked fairy-tale crap: your heart will break, your house will burn.'

When you read the story, you don't think of all these named people jamming in, but when you look at it as a writer, you have to conclude that this is a fine, heart-breaking story and a great crowd scene.

Write

Sketch out a story or scene idea involving a crowd scene or a scene involving multiple and/or interrupted dialogue. Decide whether the crowd scene is to be actual or, as in the Beattie story, suggested by references to people in the dialogue and people already present in the story or scene.

Case study: Dostoyevsky, *Crime and Punishment*

Among literal crowd scenes, one of the best known is the funeral dinner scene in Dostoyevsky's *Crime and Punishment*, published in 1866. In order to understand its particular methods of using dialogue, it's necessary to quote at some length from it: it's a scene that evolves over two chapters, it changes emotional direction, and the crowd keeps changing, too.

The dinner is given by Katerina Ivanovna, the widow of Marmeladov, a drunkard run over by a carriage. To pay for the dinner, Katerina Ivanovna, in the terminal stages of tuberculosis, has used part of the money given to her by her stepdaughter Sonia, who has impetuously been given it by the student Raskolnikov. It takes place in the one-room apartment of the impoverished Katerina Ivanovna and her three young children. The table has been well laid and the food well cooked by the landlady of the lodging house, Amalia Ivanovna, for whom Katerina Ivanovna's initial respect is quickly replaced by scorn for this 'German' who dares to think herself the equal of her, Katerina Ivanovna, the daughter of a man who was a colonel (almost a colonel) and almost governor of a province.

At first, very few people show up; many of those invited – other lodging-house inhabitants – have chosen not to come. What fills the room at this point is the description of the food and drink laid on, and the frenzy of preparations.

***

There was no great variety of wine, nor was there Madeira, but wine there was. There was vodka, rum and Lisbon wine, all of the poorest quality but in sufficient quantity. Besides the traditional rice and honey, there were three or four dishes, one of which consisted of pancakes, all prepared in Amalia Ivanovna's kitchen. Two samovars were boiling, that tea and punch might be offered after dinner.

It's the excited non-stop chatter of Katerina Ivanovna to Raskolnikov that creates the air of business and bustle. 'Could she be stuck up, the stupid German, because she was mistress of the house and had consented as a favour to help her poor lodgers! As a favour! Fancy that! Katerina Ivanovna's father who had been a colonel and almost a governor had sometimes had the table set for forty persons, and then any one like Amalia Ivanovna, or rather Ludwigovna, would not have been allowed into the kitchen.'

Despite this talk, the truth remains that beside Katerina, Amalia, and Raskolnikov, when it's time to sit down to the table, there's only one other guest: 'the Pole, a wretched looking clerk with a spotty face and a greasy coat, who had not a word to say for himself, and smelt abominably, a deaf and almost blind old man who had once been in the post office and who had been from immemorial ages maintained by someone at Amalia Ivanovna's.'

But then Dostoyevsky continues, seemingly contradicting his last statement:

***

A retired clerk of the commissariat came, too; he was drunk, had a loud and most unseemly laugh and only fancy – was without a waistcoat. One of the visitors sat straight down to the table without even greeting Katerina Ivanovna. Finally one person having no suit appeared in his dressing-gown, but this was too much, and the efforts of Amalia Ivanovna and the Pole succeeded in removing him. The Pole brought with him, however, two other Poles who did not live at Amalia Ivanovna's and whom no one had seen here before. All this irritated Katerina Ivanovna intensely. 'For whom had they made all these preparations then?' To make room for the visitors the children had not even been laid for at the table; but the two little ones were sitting on a bench in the furthest corner with their dinner laid on a box, while Polenka as a big girl had to look after them, feed them, and keep their noses wiped like well-bred children.

Note that the narration beginning 'A retired clerk' is from Katerina Ivanovna's point of view; expressions such as 'only fancy' bring this close to indirect quotation. The helter-skelter way

Dostoyevsky proceeds with listing the guests and arrivals precisely matches the disappointing beginning (only the Pole) and continues with people none of whom are 'fitting' for Katerina Ivanovna. The crowd doesn't grow so much as somehow materialize, one after the unpleasant other, while the children are forced to sit in 'the furthest corner'.

Katerina Ivanovna adds to the sense of disappointment and chaos not only by her sarcastic commentary on the guests, but by constantly breaking off from talking to cough. In her growing outrage, her talk narrates this feast of fools:

***

'It's all that cuckoo's fault! You know whom I mean? Her, her!' Katerina Ivanovna nodded towards the landlady. 'Look at her, she's making round eyes, she feels that we are talking about her and can't understand. Pfoo, the owl! Ha-ha! (Cough-cough-cough.) And what does she put on that cap for? (Cough-cough-cough.) Have you noticed that she wants every one to consider that she is patronising me and doing me an honour by being here? I asked her like a sensible woman to invite people, especially those who knew my late husband, and look at the set of fools she has brought! The sweeps! Look at that one with the spotty face. And those wretched Poles, ha-ha-ha! (Cough-cough-cough.) Not one of them has ever poked his nose in here, I've never set eyes on them. What have they come here for, I ask you? There they sit in a row. Hey, pan!' she cried suddenly to one of them, 'have you tasted the pancakes? Take some more! Have some beer! Won't you have some vodka? Look, he's jumped up and is making his bows, they must be quite starved, poor things. Never mind, let them eat! They don't make noise, anyway, though I'm really afraid for our landlady's silver spoons. ... Amalia Ivanovna!' she addressed her suddenly, almost aloud, 'if your spoons should happen to be stolen, I won't be responsible, I warn you! Ha-ha-ha!' She laughed turning to Raskolnikov, and again nodding towards the landlady, in high glee at her sally. 'She didn't understand, she didn't understand again! Look how she sits with her mouth open! An owl, a real owl! An owl in new ribbons, ha-ha-ha!'

Here her laugh turned again to an insufferable fit of coughing that lasted five minutes. Drops of perspiration stood out on her forehead and her handkerchief was stained with blood. She showed Raskolnikov the blood in silence, and as soon as she could get her breath began whispering to him again with extreme agitation and a hectic flush on her cheeks.

By now you have every right to be wondering: But where's the crowd dialogue? The answer is that it comes obliquely, first from individuals, then in violent argument as the chapter ends and the funeral dinner shifts into a different phase.

The individual who first speaks from the crowd picks up his cue from Katerina Ivanovna:

***

…with an extremely stern face she addressed Amalia Ivanovna so sharply and loudly that the latter was quite disconcerted 'not like your dressed-up draggletails whom my father would not have taken as cooks into his kitchen, and my late husband would have done them honour if he had invited them in the goodness of his heart.'

'Yes, he was fond of drink, he was fond of it, he did drink!' cried the commissariat clerk, gulping down his twelfth glass of vodka.

'My late husband certainly had that weakness, and every one knows it,' Katerina Ivanovna attacked him at once, 'but he was a kind and honourable man, who loved and respected his family. The worst of it was his good nature made him trust all sorts of disreputable people, and he drank with fellows who were not worth the sole of his shoe. Would you believe it, Rodion Romanovitch [Raskolnikov], they found a gingerbread cock in his pocket; he was dead drunk, but he did not forget the children!'

'A cock? Did you say a cock?' shouted the commissariat clerk.

After some thought, Katerina Ivanovna admits to Raskolnikov that she was, sometimes, too severe with her late husband, but, she adds, that was only to keep him off the drink.

'Yes, he used to get his hair pulled pretty often,' roared the commissariat clerk again, swallowing another glass of vodka.

'Some fools would be the better for a good drubbing, as well as having their hair pulled. I am not talking of my late husband now!' Katerina Ivanovna snapped at him.

The flush on her cheeks grew more and more marked, her chest heaved.

In another minute she would have been ready to make a scene. Many of the visitors were sniggering, evidently delighted. They began poking the commissariat clerk and whispering something to him. They were evidently trying to egg him on.

'Allow me to ask what you are alluding to,' began the clerk, 'that is to say, whose... about whom... did you say just now... But I don't care! That's nonsense! Widow! I forgive you. ... Pass!'

And he took another drink of vodka.

In the extract above, you find the first reference to crowd sound: 'Many of the visitors were sniggering...' Note also that for the first time, a crowd is literally referred to in the word 'Many'. Dostoyevsky's crowd is created through Katerina Ivanovna's perception. The crowd is *subjective*.

From this point, for the last pages of this chapter, Katerina Ivanovna's despairing anger focuses more and more on her 'foreign' landlady, Amalia Ivanovna, until even the phlegmatic Amalia takes offence and each woman expresses her anger in terms of her own father's social status until Katerina Ivanovna declares that Amalia Ivanovna probably 'never had a father', and 'if she really had one – [he] was probably some Finnish milkman.' After yet more goading from Katerina Ivanovna – 'if she dared for one moment to set her contemptible wretch of a father on a level with her papa, she, Katerina Ivanovna would tear her cap from her head and trample it under foot' – the landlady shouts that she's the mistress of the house 'and Katerina Ivanovna should leave the lodgings that minute; then she rushed for some reason to collect the silver spoons from the table. There was a great outcry and uproar, the children began crying.'

And into this scene of chaos, in comes the only rich guest of the lodging house, Luzhin, the fiancé of Raskolnikov's sister Dounia, whom Raskolnikov has vowed will never 'buy' his sister so that she can rescue her mother and Raskolnikov from their poverty, Katerina Ivanovna, believing Luzhin must be a true gentleman because of his clothes and his status, and her fantasy that he knew her father, rushes towards him and the chapter ends.

The scene continues. The next chapter opens with Katerina Ivanovna begging Luzhin to protect her: '...Remembering my father's hospitality protect these orphans. Then this:
'Allow me, madam ... Allow me.' Pyotr Petrovitch [Luzhin] waved her off.

'Your papa as you are well aware I had not the honour of knowing' (some one laughed aloud) 'and I do not intend to take part in your everlasting squabbles with Amalia Ivanovna ... I have come here to speak of my own affairs ... and I want to have a word with your step-daughter, Sofya ... Ivanovna, I think it is! Allow me to pass.'

Pyotr Petrovitch, edging by her, went to the opposite corner where Sonia was. Katerina Ivanovna remained standing where she was, as though thunderstruck. She could not understand how Pyotr Petrovitch could deny having enjoyed her father's hospitality. Though she had invented it herself, she believed in it firmly by this time. She was struck too by the businesslike, dry and even contemptuously menacing tone of Pyotr Petrovitch. All the clamour gradually died away at his entrance. Not only was this 'serious business man' strikingly incongruous with the rest of the party, but it was evident, too, that he had come upon some matter of consequence, that some exceptional cause must have brought him and that therefore something was going to happen. Raskolnikov, standing beside Sonia, moved aside to let him pass; Pyotr Petrovitch did not seem to notice him. A minute later, Lebeziatnikov, too, appeared in the doorway; he did not come in, but stood still, listening with marked interest, almost wonder, and seemed for a time perplexed.

Luzhin, one of the great shits of literature, has surreptitiously placed a folded one-hundred rouble note into Sonia's pocket earlier, in his room (observed, however, by Lebeziatnikov who happens to be sharing the lodging room). Now the scene turns into a sort of courtroom drama, where, first, Luzhin accuses Sonia of stealing the one hundred roubles – in a plot to discredit Raskolnikov's insistence that Dounia breaks off her engagement, since Luzhin can believe only that Raskolnikov knows Sonia because he's used her as a prostitute. Luzhin then has Sonia turn out her pockets to reveal the planted money. Despite Sonia and Katerina Ivanovna's denials of theft, Luzhin insists the 'evidence' of the money proves it; he then puts on an act of magnanimity, saying he won't prosecute because of his compassion. But at Luzhin's highest, Sonia's lowest moment, Lebeziatnikov steps forward and reveals what he witnessed back in his room.

The crowd during all this becomes the spectators at a trial and something more, a people's tribunal, swaying one way or the other as the case is made and then altered. When Luzhin makes his accusation, 'Complete silence reigned in the room. Even the crying children were still. Sonia stood, deadly pale, staring at Luzhin and unable to say a word. She seemed not to understand. Some seconds passed.'

Then, when Sonia says simply she knows nothing about it, Luzhin explains in detail how it happened how he kindly contributed ten roubles for the benefit of the widow Katerina Ivanovna, leaving all his money on the table. He even cites Lebeziatnikov as witness. Sonia can only repeat she knows nothing about it, and she hands back the ten roubles Luzhin donated, but he won't take it. 'Sonia looked about her. All were looking at her with such awful, stern, ironical hostile eyes. She looked at Raskolnikov ... he stood against the wall with his arms crossed, looking at her with glowing eyes.'

And through this second chapter of the funeral dinner scene, the crowd is marked by the following:

There was a buzz of loud conversation on all sides. All was in movement.

At that moment several other persons, besides Lebeziatnikov, appeared in the doorway, among them two ladies.

Exclamations arose on all sides. Raskolnikov was silent, keeping his eyes fixed on Sonia, except for an occasional rapid glance at Luzhin.

The wail of the poor, consumptive, helpless woman seemed to produce a great effect on her audience.

Pyotr Petrovitch gave a positive start – all noticed it and recalled it afterwards. Lebeziatnikov strode into the room.

Lebeziatnikov was almost breathless. Exclamations arose on all hands, chiefly expressive of wonder, but some were threatening in tone. They all crowded around Pyotr Petrovitch. Katerina Ivanovna flew to Lebeziatnikov.

...But his [Lebeziatnikov's] speech produced a powerful effect. He had spoken with such vehemence, with such conviction that every one obviously believed him.

Pyotr Petrovitch felt that things were going badly with him.

But this retort did not benefit Pyotr Petrovitch. Murmurs of disapproval were heard on all sides.

He [Raskolnikov] appeared to be firm and composed. Every one felt clearly from the very look of him that he really knew about it and that the mystery would be solved.

It was this, or somewhat like this, that Raskolnikov wound up his speech which was followed very attentively; though often interrupted by exclamations from his audience. But in spite of interruptions he spoke clearly, calmly, exactly, firmly.

His decisive voice, his tone of conviction and his stern face made a great impression on every one.

[From this point, Luzhin knows he's been revealed as a lying cheat.]

Luzhin smiled contemptuously and did not speak. Very pale. He seemed to be deliberating on some means of escape. Perhaps he would have been glad to give up everything and get away, but at the moment this was scarcely possible. It would have implied admitting the truth of the accusations brought against him.

Moreover the company, which had already been excited by drink, was now too much stirred to allow it. The commissariat clerk, though indeed he had not grasped the whole position, was shouting louder than any one and was making some suggestions very unpleasant to Luzhin. But not all those present were drunk; lodgers came in from all the rooms. The three Poles were tremendously excited and were continually shouting at him: 'The pan is a lajdak!' and muttering threats in Polish.

Raskolnikov was attempting to speak again, but they did not let him. Every one was crowding around Luzhin with threats and shouts of abuse.

The scene and chapter end with the landlady Amalia Ivanovna throwing Katerina Ivanovna and her children out, there and then. Katerina Ivanovna rushes into the street, screaming that she will get justice; the three children crouch terrified on the trunk in the corner waiting for her return, and 'Amalia Ivanovna raged about the room, shrieking, lamenting and throwing everything she came across on the floor. The lodgers talked incoherently, some commented to the best of their ability on what had happened, others quarrelled and swore at one another, while others struck up a song.'

Focus point

The sense of crowd dialogue can be achieved with sparing, individual voices coming to the fore at moments of dramatic significance.

How are crowd scenes and dialogue explicitly presented?

So far, the examples of crowd dialogue have been oblique or more suggested than explicit. But in Charles Dickens's *Barnaby Rudge*, published in 1841, the historical setting of the Gordon Riots of 1789 in London demanded a vivid explicitness in its crowd scenes.

Here is the mob coming together, having marched quietly, as it converges on Parliament:

It was between two and three o'clock in the afternoon when the three great parties met at Westminster, and, uniting into one huge mass, raised a tremendous shout. This was not only done in token of their presence, but as a signal to those on whom the task devolved, that it was time to take possession of both Houses, and of the various avenues of approach, and of the gallery stairs. To the last named place, Hugh and Dennis, still with their pupil [Barnaby] between them, rushed straightway: Barnaby having given his flag into the hands of one of their party, who kept them at the outer door. Their followers pressing on behind, they were borne as on a great wave to the very doors of the gallery, whence it was impossible to retreat, even if they had been so inclined, by reason of the throng which choked up the passages. It is a familiar expression in describing a great crowd, that a person might have walked upon the people's heads. In this case it was actually done; for a boy who had by some means got among the concourse, and was in imminent danger of suffocation, climbed to the shoulders of a man beside him and walked upon the people's hats and heads into the open street; traversing in his passage the whole length of two staircases and a long gallery. Nor was the swarm without less dense; for a basket which had been tossed into the crowd, was jerked from head to head, and shoulder to shoulder, and went spinning and whirling on above them, until it was lost to view, without ever once falling in among them or coming near the ground.

Through this vast throng, sprinkled doubtless here and there with honest zealots, but composed for the most part of the very scum and refuse of London, whose growth was fostered by bad criminal laws, bad prison regulations, and the worst conceivable police, such of the members of both Houses of Parliament as had not taken the precaution to be already at their posts, were compelled to fight and force their way. Their carriages were stopped and broken; the wheels wrenched off; the glasses shivered to atoms; the panels beaten in; drivers, footmen, and masters, pulled from their seats and rolled in the mud.

Lords, commoners, and reverend bishops, with little distinction of person or party, were kicked and pinched and hustled; passed from hand to hand through various stages of ill-usage; and sent to their fellow-senators at last with their clothes hanging in ribands about them, their bigwigs torn off, themselves speechless and breathless, and their persons covered with the powder which had been cuffed and beaten out of their hair.

One Lord was so long in the hands of the populace, that the Peers as a body resolved to sally forth and rescue him, and were in the act of doing so, when he happily appeared among them covered with dirt and bruises, and hardly to be recognized by those who knew him best. The noise and uproar were on the increase every moment. The air was filled with execrations, hoots, and howlings. The mob raged and roared, like a mad monster as it was, unceasingly, and each new outrage served to swell its fury.

Inside Parliament 'the tumult both within and without was so great, that those who attempted to speak could scarcely hear their own voices: far less, consult upon the course it would be wise to take in such extremity, or animate each other to dignified and firm resistance.' This continues:

...So sure as any member, just arrived, with dress disordered and dishevelled hair, came struggling through the crowd in the lobby, it yelled and screamed in triumph; and when the door of the House, partially and continuously opened by those within for his admission, gave them a momentary glimpse of the interior, they grew more wild and savage, like beasts of prey, and made a rush against the portal which strained its locks and bolts in their staples, and shook the very beams.

The mob here is presented as making a great many sounds, but none as direct speech. It's only when an individual commander speaks to the crowd, or a portion of it, that the crowd response is presented as speech.

'Order!' cried Hugh, in a voice which made itself heard even above the roar and tumult, as Lord George appeared at the top of the staircase. 'News! News from my lord!'

The noise continued, notwithstanding his appearance, until Gashford looked around.

There was silence immediately – even among the people in the passages without, and on the other staircases, who could neither see nor hear, but to whom, notwithstanding, the signal was conveyed with marvellous rapidity.

'Gentlemen,' said Lord George, who was very pale and agitated, 'we must be firm.

They talk of delays, but we must have no delays. They talk of taking your petition into consideration next Tuesday, but we must have it considered now. Present appearances look bad for our success, but we must succeed and will!"

'We must succeed and will!' echoed the crowd. And so among their shouts and cheers and other cries, he bowed to them and retired...

This convention that the crowd when it speaks will speak in one voice – or one slogan it has picked up from its leader – is an old convention of crowd speech. Another, which Dickens doesn't use here, is to give the readers a series of individual voices from within the crowd representing 'their shouts and cheers and other cries'.

As in *Barnaby Rudge*, the crowd is often most vividly represented by focusing on several known characters within it, as when the dim-witted Barnaby is put at the head of one of the three huge sections of the mob converging on Westminster. Then dialogue between characters can arise, as it were, from the narrative describing the crowd of which they're part, and leave reader imagination to fill in a background noise which may contain much other dialogue taking place simultaneously.

 Key idea

The dialogue of a crowd is either a mass chant, song or response, or individual voices in dialogue with each other while within the crowd and/ or calling out from the crowd.

Focus points

This chapter has looked at how interrupted speech and multiple speech can be represented in writing, and how a crowd and its voices can be either suggested or explicitly represented. The chapter's main ideas are summarized in the following five points:

- It is literally impossible to read two or more voices overlapping or speaking different words at the same time. Various conventions of layout and punctuation can be used. But most important is the explanation of what is to take place through direct narrative or a character's dialogue.

- Interruptions are conventionally signalled by a dash replacing end punctuation to indicate the direct speech of one character being broken off by the speech of another. This break can be written to make the connection of the successive statements, unintended by the characters, contribute comic or other significant qualities of tone to the scene.

- Multiple speech is often signified by the same 'broken off' convention of a dash as end punctuation in a character's dialogue. However, this requires narrative and/or dialogue exposition prior to the onset of the multiple dialogue. Readers will be willing to make the imaginative effort if the writer makes it worth the try.

- Powerful effects of tone, character and theme can be created by the suggestion of a crowd whose dialogue is inferred from character reaction in reflection, whether in narration of thought or in the character's direct dialogue. Another way a real crowd can be evoked is by one or two main characters in the scene frequently referring to it or to one or more of its members. This can be augmented by individual voices from the crowd responding to the main characters.

- The conventional crowd speaks explicitly only in mass chant, song, or response to individual leaders addressing it. Individual voices may be heard rising from the crowd to express complementary or contradictory points of view. Dialogue between individuals within the crowd can help develop an expression of the crowd mood, views and reactions to events of its own making or to others who may be onlookers or authorities of control.

Next step

Chapter 8 looks at various examples of representing foreign dialogue in fiction and the strategies behind them.

8

Dialogue in foreign languages; accents and dialect

In this chapter you will learn:

- The reasons for including or excluding foreign-language dialogue in English language fiction
- How foreign-language dialogue can develop plot and character
- How to present foreign-language dialogue in a realistic way
- How to represent accents and dialects.

What is the point of having foreign dialogue in fiction written in English?

Short answer: The question isn't as dumb as it appears.

First, there are always reasons. You may have a character or characters who speak little or no English. Your setting may be in a non-English speaking place. You may have characters speak a foreign language as means of privacy, secrecy or exclusion.

Nevertheless, none of these necessitates dialogue in a foreign language. The more compelling, encompassing reason for having foreign dialogue or not having foreign dialogue is because of your authorial decision.

In the opening pages of her novel *Death Comes for the Archbishop*, Willa Cather announces her intention. The setting is Rome in 1848, and the characters are three cardinals and an American bishop. Cather, in omniscient third-person narration, writes, 'The language spoken was French – the time had already gone when Cardinals could conveniently discuss contemporary matters in Latin.' One page later, the first dialogue statement occurs.

> The Bishop laughed and threw out his brown hands in apology. 'Likely enough I have forgot my manners. I am preoccupied.'

Cather has told you they are speaking in French, but when they finally speak, it's in English. Cather hasn't made a mistake. She's used the convention of announcing the actual language spoken and then presented it in the language of the novel – English. It is possible, among other reasons, that the page of narrative between the announcement of French being spoken and the dialogue appearing in English helps you forget the artifice of the convention.

This represents one way you can indicate a foreign language is being spoken without using a word of that language in the dialogue. Cather clearly didn't want to write an entire scene of dialogue in French.

It also raises the question:

Why would you want to avoid using a foreign language?

Of course you're writing in English, but you could have some foreign dialogue within your English writing. Your reasons for not doing so might be formal: some structural decision makes you keep all the writing English. It might be a function of your narrative point of view, a first-person narrator who doesn't speak the foreign language, or a limited omniscient narration with the same linguistic limitation. It might be your more personal interpretation of realism: you don't speak the foreign language so it's more practical and/or honest to keep it out of the dialogue you write.

Key idea

The inclusion/exclusion of foreign dialogue, when character or setting make it possible, is your authorial decision.

What would a high degree of foreign-language dialogue realism look like?

Here's how Cormac McCarthy presents it in *All the Pretty Horses*:

> They stood in the kitchen with their hats in their hands, and the gerente sat at the table and studied them.
>
> Amansadores, he said.
>
> Sí.
>
> Ambos, he said.
>
> Sí. Ambos.
>
> He leaned back. He drummed his fingers on the metal table top.
>
> Hay dieseis caballos en il postero, said John Grady. Podemas amansarlos en cuatro días.

McCarthy is being realistic and logically consistent. The novel is narrated in English, so when Spanish is spoken by any character, the identifying narration remains in English. Without having to know Spanish, the readers will know that John Grady and his non-Spanish speaking friend Rawlins have gone to the ranch kitchen to talk about their offer to break in sixteen penned wild horses in four days, an improbably difficult feat to achieve. If the readers can make out any of the words such as 'dieseis' (sixteen), or 'cuatro' (four), they can deduce what is being said. And if they can't? Might this dialogue in a foreign language bore them? Confuse them? Irritate them?

It might. On the other hand, hyper-realism isn't what McCarthy is after. The novel is, on one level, a wonderful inversion of the conventional idea of the Mexican as the poor, illegal immigrant to the United States. Its central character, John Grady, is a poor, illegal American immigrant in Mexico, appreciated for his horsemanship, but looked down on socially and quickly assumed to be guilty of crime. So the 'untranslated' Spanish gives readers the sense of what it is to try to live in a foreign place *in a foreign language*. And this contributes to this inverted point of view. It's a brilliant device, and the Spanish never goes on too long. It's often translated by John Grady to the non-Spanish speakers with him.

 Write

> Take a dialogue scene you've written (for one of these exercises or otherwise) and set it in a foreign country. Justify your choice of using or not using foreign dialogue in the scene.

Immediately following the Spanish conversation in the ranch kitchen, John Grady and Rawlins leave.

> They walked back across the yard to the bunkhouse to wash for supper.
>
> What did he say? Said Rawlins.
>
> He said we were full of shit. But in a nice way.

Giving one character the ability to translate for another opens up many possible dialogues. Here, John Grady light-heartedly reinterprets what was said to him, but does give Rawlins the answer to his question. Earlier in the novel, when he and Rawlins were travelling with the slightly simple-minded troublemaker Blevins, a group of Mexicans they come across ask John Grady if he'll sell Blevins to them. When Blevins asks what the men said, John Grady tells him they said nothing, rather than tell the truth and frighten or aggravate this misfit companion.

A great deal of plot and character potential inheres in the translator(s) of foreign dialogue within the fiction.

 Key idea

> The decision to use foreign dialogue brings new potential to character and plot development in fiction.

Write

Write a short scene in which your character engages in foreign dialogue. (Never mind if you don't speak another language. Write it in English and pretend it's a foreign language.) Then have your character translate or paraphrase it accurately to the non-foreign language speaker with them. Do this again, but with your character distorting it to the companion – for a reason significant to character, relationship and, potentially, plot.

Case study: Hemingway and foreign-language dialogue

Ernest Hemingway's fiction offers a casebook of what has come to be standard modern ways of representing foreign-language dialogue either by direct identifying narrative or in a variety of indirect ways. Hemingway had to deal with this since so much of his fiction – short stories as well as novels – has non-English speaking settings. Typically, the foreign languages are Spanish, Italian or French. German appears on occasion. The focus in this Case study is on Hemingway's short stories; their foreign-language representations cover those used in his novels.

In 'Another Country', the foreign dialogue becomes the topic of conversation between the Italian major and the American narrator.

…One day I had said that Italian seemed such an easy language to me that I could not take a great interest in it; everything was so easy to say. 'Ah, yes,' the major said. 'Why, then, do you not take up the use of grammar?' So we took up the use of grammar, and soon Italian was such a difficult language that I was afraid to talk to him until I had the grammar straight in my mind.

The formal tone of the major's question is one of the key ways Hemingway used to indicate dialogue in a foreign language. 'Why, then, do you not take up the use of grammar?' is not the same as 'Then why don't you speak it grammatically?' The latter would be the more conversational representation.

In 'Hills Like White Elephants', two other methods of indicating foreign dialogue are used.

First, early in the conversation in English between the American man and the girl:

***

'It's pretty hot,' the man said.
'Let's drink beer.'
'Dos cervezas,' the man said into the curtain.
'Big ones?' a woman asked from the doorway.
'Yes. Two big ones.'

The man, ordering the beer, switches to Spanish. The Spanish woman's reply is in English, representing her ordinary Spanish conversation. This exchange isn't the simplest representation of language being changed.

The next time Spanish is used, half a page along, the switch is clearer:

***

'We want two Anis del Toro.' [The man says.]
'Do you want it with water?' [The woman says.]
'Do you want it with water?'
'I don't know,' the girl said. 'Is it good with water?'

This technique, the repetition of the question to the non-Spanish speaker, is much clearer. The man is speaking English to the girl. He was speaking Spanish to the woman, and everything has been represented in English dialogue.

Therefore, after the man then answers the girl's question by saying, 'It's all right' with water, the following two lines of dialogue are immediately understood by readers to be in Spanish.
'You want them with water?' asked the woman.
'Yes, with water.'

Hemingway uses another way of indicating foreign dialogue in this story.

***

The woman came out through the curtains with two glasses of beer and put them down on the damp felt pads.
'The train comes in five minutes,' she said.
'What did she say?' asked the girl.
'That the train is coming in five minutes.'

You know by now that the woman speaks in Spanish, so the girl asks because she doesn't understand Spanish. Note, too, that Hemingway doesn't literally repeat the woman's words. The man answers in a clause that alters the verb from 'comes' to 'is coming'. This serves to suggest the change in language.

It's also worth noting that, after the man's initial order for two beers in Spanish, there is no more Spanish dialogue presented in Spanish in the story. If you know this classic short story, you understand that this contributes to the couple's social isolation as foreigners alone in their own language, and the monolingual girl even more so.

Key idea

Choosing to present foreign dialogue in its language or to present it in English is a decision dependent on the intention of mood and meaning in the fiction.

Write

Take one of your scenes, set it in a foreign (non-English speaking) place, and decide how much of the foreign dialogue should appear in its original language, how much in English, and how much implied. (Implied would be like: 'Jim said the headwaiter told him we'd have to wait forty-five minutes for a table.') Make your choice relevant to the mood and meaning of your scene.

Case study: Hemingway (continued)

In Hemingway's story 'Che Ti Dice La Patria', set in 1930s Italy, a young Fascist insists on being given a lift in a two-seater car with two men already in it. He hops on the running-board and holds on to the inside of the car. When he's finally dropped off, he asks how much he owes for the ride.

***

'Nothing.'
'Why not?'
'I don't know,' I said.
'Then thanks,' the young man said, not 'thank you,' or 'thank

you very much,' or 'thank you a thousand times,' all of which you formerly said in Italy to a man when he handed you a time-table or explained about a direction. The young man uttered the lowest form of the word 'thanks' and looked after us suspiciously as Guy started the car. I waved my hand at him. He was too dignified to reply.

All the dialogue has taken place in Italian, which has been signalled earlier by the young man who, when told 'You will be uncomfortable,' replies, 'That makes nothing,' a literal translation of Italian (and other languages) idiom for 'That doesn't matter' (idiomatic English) and by Guy asking the Italian-speaking narrator what the Fascist has said. But Hemingway can't make the point about the rude arrogance of the young man simply by having him say 'Thanks', which in an English-language context can be polite and sincere. So the first-person narrator explains the nuances of thanking someone in Italian for the meaning to be made clear. Even if he'd put it in Italian as 'grazie', only readers who know Italian would get it. Might get it. There's no way around this: you sometimes will have to explain the subtler meaning of foreign dialogue in whatever language it appears. The point is that Hemingway links this with the unpleasant social changes present in the story during this particular time and place.

Later, the narrator and Guy are having lunch at a sleazy café in La Spezia where the waitresses are also prostitutes.

***

'You like me?' she asked Guy.
'He adores you,' I said. 'But he doesn't speak Italian.'
'Ich spreche Deutsch,' she said, and stroked Guy's hair.
'Speak to the lady in your native tongue, Guy.'
'Where do you come from?' asked the lady.
'Potsdam.'
'And you will stay here now for a little while?'
'In this so dear Spezia?' I asked.
'Tell her we have to go,' said Guy. 'Tell her we have no money.'
'My friend is a misogynist,' I said, 'an old German misogynist.'

Here. Hemingway uses Guy's lack of Italian and German to enliven an otherwise depressing afternoon.

Foreign dialogue can certainly be used for comic/ironic purpose when one or more characters don't understand it.

In a very short story, 'A Simple Enquiry', Hemingway uses yet another variation of representing foreign dialogue. He has an officer's adjutant reply 'Yes, signor maggiore.' They are speaking to each other in Italian that is represented in English. But rather than write 'Yes, major, sir,' Hemingway presents the address to the officer in Italian, since the address substitutes for the major's name, which is of course an Italian name. So the 'Yes' stays in English because that's the only part of the statement that isn't naming the officer. And when the officer calls for his adjutant, he replies, 'Signor maggiore?', the entire reply being this equivalent of a proper name.

A similar technique, using German, occurs in 'An Alpine Idyll', in which two American skiers come down off the mountain into an inn and are greeted with the innkeeper's 'Ski-heil!' Their response of 'Heil!' establishes that the dialogue is in German. The innkeeper then asks, 'How was it up above?', to which one of the skiers replies 'Schön. A little too much sun.' The shift from German to English spoken between the skiers involves first a word in German but is mostly signalled by a shift from a formal to informal level of diction.

They order beer while they open their mail.

***

A girl brought it in this time. She smiled as she opened the bottles.
'Many letters,' she said.
'Yes. Many.'
'Prosit,' she said and went out, taking the empty bottles.
'I'd forgotten what beer tasted like.'
'I hadn't,' John said...

The shift in diction – the simple contraction of 'I had' to 'I'd' and the response with the informal contraction of 'hadn't' rather than 'had not' – tells you they're speaking English.

Although standard German is understood by the skiers, when a nonstandard German that they can't understand is used, it is noted in the narrative and isn't represented in English: 'The innkeeper came in and went over to the table. He spoke in dialect and the sexton answered him.' When the innkeeper wants the sexton to share his story with the skiers, Hemingway writes, 'You go on and tell it,' he said to the sexton. 'Speak German, not dialect.' Hemingway takes care to be realistic without overcomplicating multilingual dialogue.

Focus point

It's better to state a second or further language change in narrative than to overcomplicate the dialogue (unless linguistic confusion is your aim).

Case study: Hemingway (continued)

In Hemingway's justly celebrated story 'A Clean, Well-Lighted Place', the dialogue is only signalled as foreign by its slightly formal tone and, perhaps, by a few indications of social setting. Not until its end section does a foreign word enter, in the exchange: 'Are you trying to insult me?' 'No, hombre, only to make a joke.' So you probably know from this that the dialogue is in Spanish. But if you don't know Spanish at all, what can you make of the following interior dialogue (monologue) of the older waiter, the story's central character, which is the story's emotional climax?

***

...It was not fear or dread. It was a nothing that he knew too well. It was all a nothing and a man was nothing too. It was only that and light was all it needed and a certain cleanness and order. Some lived in it and never felt it but he knew it was all nada y pues nada y nada y pues nada. Our nada who art in nada, nada be they name thy kingdom nada thy will be nada as it is in nada. Give us this nada our daily nada and nada us our nada as we nada our nadas and nada us not into nada but deliver us from nada, pues nada. Hail nothing full of nothing, nothing is with thee.

If you don't figure it out, you haven't been paying attention. Hemingway had done all the identifying work required. He begins by repeating 'nothing' and then repeats 'nada' and then, for good measure, goes back to repeating 'nothing'.

Focus point

Trust your feelings about foreign dialogue, and never assume your readers are stupid.

Case study: Hemingway (continued)

For the most part, Hemingway's foreign dialogue in novels as well as short stories is indicated by a slightly to very formal level of diction and an occasional literal translation of foreign idiom into English, such as 'That makes nothing' for 'It doesn't matter' or 'That doesn't mean anything'.

In the story 'A Way You'll Never Be', Captain Paravicini says to Nick, 'We made a very fine attack. Truly. A very fine attack. I will show you. Look.' If you were asked to write this content ten different ways in English, you wouldn't come up with these words in this order. It's simply not conversational, idiomatic English.

In 'Homage to Switzerland', Hemingway's most structurally experimental story, a character, a waitress, is using foreign dialogue – English.

***

'The Express is an hour late, sir,' she said. 'Can I bring you some coffee?'

'If it's not too much trouble.'

'Please?' asked the waitress.

'I'll take some.'

'Thank you.'

She brought the coffee from the kitchen and Mr. Johnson looked out the window at the snow falling in the light from the station platform.

'Do you speak other languages besides English?' he asked the waitress.

'Oh, yes, I speak German and French and the dialects.'

She speaks English, but not idiomatic English, so she doesn't understand his 'If it's not too much trouble.' His second response is in non-idiomatic English, but in a translation of the foreign-language idiom, which she understands, at which she thanks him. Johnson is therefore having a bit of a private joke when he asks if she speaks languages *other* than English. He next calls the waitress back with 'Signorina!' Another little joke, since Italian is not one of the languages she's said she speaks.

Johnson is horsing around with languages to distract him from thinking of his recent divorce, his wife having walked out on him. At one point, when he's bought champagne for the railway porters and sits drinking with them, Hemingway writes:

***

'None of you gentlemen is divorced?' Johnson asked. He had stopped clowning with the language and was speaking good French now and had been for some time.

It could be that in longer pieces of fiction, the shift into seriousness and 'good' French could be gradually achieved through the dialogue itself, but the short story justifies the direct narrative statement.

Finally, the plot of 'The Gambler, The Nun, and the Radio' requires the presence of an interpreter between a Spanish-speaking Mexican witness/victim of a crime and the non-Spanish speaking American police officer. Hemingway makes the scene more interesting by having the Mexican understand more English than he lets on to the police, and by having an interpreter with a mind and sympathies of his own.

The Mexican told the police he had no idea who shot him. He believed it to be an accident.
'An accident that he fired eight shots at you and hit you twice, there?'
'Si, senor,' said the Mexican, who was named Cayetano Ruiz.
'An accident that he hit me at all, the cabron,' he said to the interpreter.
'What does he say?' asked the detective sergeant, looking across the bed at the interpreter.
'He says it was an accident.'
'Tell him to tell the truth, that he is going to die,' the detective said.
'No,' said Cayetano. 'But tell him that I feel very sick and would prefer not to talk so much.'
'He says that he is telling the truth,' the interpreter said. Then speaking confidentially to the detective, 'He don't know who shot him. They shot him in the back.'
'Yes,' said the detective. 'I understand that, but why did the bullets all go in the front?'
'Maybe he is spinning around,' said the interpreter.

Interpreters can certainly open up new vistas of dialogue for writers. Though this story is serious, much of its surface is comic, and much of that comedy is in unconventional dialogue – from the witness and his protective interpreter as well as from a nursing nun who prays for the Notre Dame football team to win its games and who very, very much wants to become a saint.

Focus point

You can use English itself as a foreign language in identifying those who don't speak it well, or idiomatically, or as a first language.

Should you try to represent foreign accents?

Yes, if you must, but sparingly. If you write 'Ve vant Villiam Vallace to vin', your readers will snigger even if you don't want them to.

In a first draft of a novel, I had two recent Cuban immigrants to the United States as major secondary characters. I was quite proud of the spellings I'd invented to give them very accurate Cuban accents in English. I gave the MS to a friend, a retired literary editor, to read. His verdict was that it wasn't a bad story, but he couldn't understand a single word either of the Cubans said. I threw them out of the book. I liked their accents so much I'd given the pair far too much development to the detriment of major characters.

For educated characters, a slightly too formal English can indicate foreignness. This, combined with knowing where they're from, can suggest enough so that readers can fill in just the right accent. Another possible technique with foreigners intent on learning English is to have them ask a question or two about idiom. But not often.

It is sometimes enough to describe a foreign pronunciation and leave it to the reader to hear it.

Several of these techniques occur in my novel *Wolf Tones*, as its central character, Ethan Baum, introduces himself, rather unwillingly, to Stucic, the man in the next seat on the airplane as they fly to Albuquerque, New Mexico.

…'You are from Albuquerque?' Stucic asks, putting an extra syllable between his rolled 'r' and the 'q.'

'I will be. I'm going to teach at the University.' Ethan wonders is the pretentiousness of 'I will be' is linked to the precariousness of his job.

Stucic says, 'Aha. I, too, Eaten. It is Eaten, as in Frome?'

'Exactly. Ethan.'

'Eee-than,' says Stucic, sticking out his tongue.

And though Stucic is a major secondary character, this is the first and last description of how he sounds. The simple inversion of 'Are you from Albuquerque?' to "You are from Albuquerque?" creates the sense, the sound, of foreignness.

In another novel, a minor character, a recent Russian immigrant to New York, is given foreign-sounding dialogue in other ways. He's not highly educated like Stucic, though he's very intelligent. He speaks in fast torrents which carry with them a tangle of mixed metaphor and confused clichés. And, like many Slavic speakers of English, he tends to drop definite and indefinite articles indiscriminately. He also loses prepositions. What he strives for is to somehow sound up-to-the-minute hip. That he may well roll his *r*s and put slight *y* sounds before some vowels and pronounce short *i*s like long *e*s is never stated. So the readers may or may not hear them in the character's dialogue. If they don't, that's preferable to over-elaborated 'new' spellings, or to slowing down the dialogue with narrative explanations of its sound. Here are some examples of his voice: (In full manic flow on voice message.)

'Three-two-one-six, hello boss is what we spend fix up the place. You like? If no is all refundable and we can go upmarket jiggedy-jog. Maybe I'm back there tonight with pictures from Upper East Hayes. Suggest, boss, anyhow you take a look before what next. Also get more bad news from a contact I hope you should never meet...'

(The character's name is Abrasha Addison; the surname is suspect. Here he tries to help his boss, Schwartz, out of a mess that he, Abrasha, has created by trying to do a fast deal on faux furniture.)

Addison, putting down the phone in unison with Schwartz, yelled, 'What kind no good stinking pahologist liar this Simpkins?'

'Very funny, Addison. Let that be a lesson to you in efficiency. It took me just three minutes to wipe out ten days' work. Is that you coming up through Mock-Mahogany Gulch?'

'Never mind, boss. Be of faint heart. We keep plugging along a finger in every dike, we pull out some plums.'

'And say what a good boy... Good-bye, Abrasha. Take the rest of the day off, all eight minutes.'

Addison tapped his shoulder. 'Don't be silly. I go now to sell this furniture, move it out tomorrow, lunch is latest. But is too disgusting crowded you sleep here tonight. You come to Brighton Beach, then we have nice dinner – Georgian, Uzbecki, Moldavian – what you want. I have good extra bed.'

(Later, they've moved office.)

Schwartz killed time, fidgeted. The case was making him a whiz of a fidget, a maniacally busy do-nothing. If Addison only knew.

At five to noon, Addison announced he'd be finished with the bookkeeping in five minutes.

'How can you work so exactly?'

'What exactly? I'm screwing around like you, make thirty minutes' work go two and a half hours. You think in Odessa we don't learn good American business practice?'

Addison's is of course an exaggerated voice, but he is based on a number of new Russian/Ukrainian immigrant voices I'd heard.

Following are examples of various accents in English, in dialect, and from immigrant and ethnic groups. All are examples of how it should be done.

Lana Turner they discovered at the Schraft counter, me on a bench for the Wilshire bus. Claire hired me for nanny, live-in, without even asking a reference. When I first came the house, I was surprised, because it is small small. Normal touches a mother would do, I did not see here. Pictures, they left just leaning against the walls. The living room looked like a school, books everywhere and a telescope by the front window. Good, I thought, Lola will learn.

(Lola, a Filipina nanny, one of the narrators in Mona Simpson's *My Hollywood*, a foreign voice created with minimal changes from standard English.)

'Ahright, Tukks?'

'Coco-head bwoy, ahright?'

'Yeh, yeh, yeh!'

'Yeh, yeh!'

'An' she to 'member to use her ole chemise for your nex' shirt.'

> (James Berry, writing of Jamaican village life in 'A Thief in the Village'.)

He lifted himself, kneeled beside her a moment, kissed the inner side of her thighs, then drew down her skirts, buttoning his own clothes unthinking, not even turning aside, in the faint, faint light from the lantern.

'Tha mun come ter th' cottage one time,' he said, looking down at her with a warm, sure, easy face.

> (D.H. Lawrence's dialect for the gamekeeper in *Lady Chatterley's Lover*.)

What? Goddom! Goddom it! I never think he be as poor as dat!

Settin at shadders, way out dere!

Sailin to dese reefs

All de days of his life, and den he go and set his net out dere –

Dat mon can't learn nothing from de sea. Dat mon

> (The voice of a Cayman Islands fisherman in *Far Tortuga*, by Peter Matthiessen.)

'What, then? Don't get pitiful. I won't stand for you getting pitiful, hear me?'

'We born around the same time, me and you,' said Violet. 'We women, me and you. Tell me something real. Don't just say I'm grown and ought to know. I'm fifty and I don't know nothing. What about it? Do I stay with him? I want to, I think. I want… well, I didn't always… now I want. I want some fat in this life.'

> (Dialogue between two black women in New York City, from *Jazz*, by Toni Morrison.)

'Can you tell me something? To your mind, does the British Museum rate more highly than the National Gallery? Or would you recommend gallery over museum?'

The conductor pushed his lower lip out with his tongue. He stared hard at Chanu, as if considering whether to eject him from the bus.

'In my rating system,' explained Chanu, 'they are neck and neck. It would be good to take an opinion from a local.'

> (Dialogue of a middle-aged man from Bangladesh, a long-time resident in London, from Monica Ali's *Brick Lane*.)

 ## Key idea

In writing dialogue in dialect or with any kind of accent, make the fewest possible changes to ordinary spelling. If you must change it, make sure it's fairly obvious how the word(s) should be pronounced.

Focus points

This chapter has examined ways of representing foreign language in dialogue and how accents and dialects can be represented. Its main ideas are summarized in the following five points:

- Your fiction is in English, but your decision on how to represent non-English dialogue within it is dependent, finally, on your authorial decision. Considerations of narrative point of view will always play some part in reaching that decision.

- When you have foreign dialogue in your fiction, it brings new potential such as which characters speak or understand the language, and whether it's translated for them accurately by a character or, for any of a variety of reasons, distorted.

- The decision to present a foreign dialogue in its original language or in English is often a function of the mood and content of the scene.

- It's better to state a change of language in your narrative than to overcomplicate the foreign dialogue's representation in English.

- In writing dialogue with foreign accent or regional dialect, keep changes from standard spelling to a minimum, and make all necessary changes as simple and clearly pronounceable as you can.

Next step

Chapter 9 looks at extremes of dialogue in terms of characters who can't use standard thought and/or expression, formal strictures imposed on composition, and the removal of boundaries between thought and dialogue.

The further reaches of dialogue

In this chapter you will learn:

- About extreme or unusual dialogue
- How unconventional dialogue can be used to represent social, physical or psychological conditions
- How unconventional dialogue can arise from the setting of your work (e.g. science fiction or fantasy)
- How extreme or unusual dialogue can arise from self-imposed conditions (e.g. writing without using the letter 'e')
- About removing the boundaries between thought and speech.

The dialogue referred to in this chapter is structured differently from that in the rest of the book. The reasons for the differences have to do with either the special nature of the characters to whom it is given, the special circumstances of setting in place and time, or the particular formal constraints set on the writing. Another difference is due to intentional ambiguity in separation between thought and dialogue.

Particular examples of the demand of setting and time could be a technologically based language as in some science fiction, or language based on myth and legend, as in fantasy fiction. It might be special language in the service of satire, as in various sections of *Gulliver's Travels*, or language for animals as in *Watership Down* (though it's the former book that has the most perfectly created word for horses, Houyhnhnms, that near-as-damnit imitation of a whinny). But most of science fiction and fantasy fiction have dialogue well within the range discussed in earlier chapters.

Less usual dialogue may be based on character: psychotic or brain-damaged characters might have distorted speech or obsessive speech, speech of limited vocabulary or a form of private language. Characters might also share a private language, such as siblings who develop a language to exclude all others.

Specific, unusual speech may be created for formal reasons, for example, if you decided, like Georges Perec, to write an entire novel (in French) without using the letter *e*. This formal constraint of omission is called a lipogram. Perec's 1969 novel was entitled *La Disparation*, which could ordinarily translate as *The Disappearance*, or *The Death*, but which, sticking to the same compositional rule, was translated into English as *A Void*.

Though the language of 'mad' people certainly occurs in the earliest fiction – Cervantes' eponymous Don Quixote is, though moving and meaningful, certainly mad. However, his speech, used to describe his visions and delusions, is not itself mad; it is merely antiquely chivalric and subsequently out of place and time.

The first fiction to *show* the onset of madness as the degeneration of rationality in speech is probably Nikolai Gogol's 1835 story 'The Diary of a Madman'. The story consists of 19 diary entries. The first ten are dated from 3 October to 8 December, with no year given. The eleventh entry is dated 'Year 2000, April 43'. The following entries are: 'Martober 86, Between day and night', 'No date. A day without date', 'Can't remember the day. Nor was there a month', 'Damned if I know what's been going on' and, finally, 'da 34 te Mnth. Yr. yraurbef 349'.

This diary of a minor Russian civil servant begins sanely enough. The diarist (never named) begins with an account of waking late for work one day. He knows he'll be treated unpleasantly by his Chief when he arrives and he explains how mean his department is compared to others, yet he says he stays on because his department has the greatest prestige. On the way to work he sees the carriage of the Department Director and sees the Director's daughter step from it and go into a clothing store, leaving her lapdog Madgie in the rain. So far, so normal. He then hears a little voice say 'Hello, Madgie.' He looks around but no one's there. Two ladies have passed him. Then he hears, behind him, the same little voice saying 'You ought to be ashamed, Madgie.'

What on earth was going on? I saw Madgie and a dog that had been following the two ladies sniffing at one another. 'Maybe I'm drunk,' I said to myself, 'but it's not likely. It doesn't happen to me very often.' 'No, Fidele, you're wrong.' With my own eyes I saw Madgie forming the words. 'I was, bow-wow, I was, bow-wow, very sick.' Talk about a lapdog! I must say I was quite surprised to hear her talking. Later, however, when I had properly sized up the situation, I was no longer surprised. ...But I'll confess that I was much more bewildered when Madgie said: 'I *did* write you, Fidele. Perhaps Fido didn't give you my letter.' Now, I'd be willing to forfeit a month's pay if I've ever heard of a dog that could write. Only a gentleman can write correctly anyway. Of course, one finds some scribbling shopkeepers – even serfs – but that sort of writing is mostly mechanical; no commas, periods, or spelling. So I was surprised. I'll confess that recently I have been seeing and hearing things that no one else has seen or heard. 'Let's,' I said to myself, 'follow this little dog [Fidele] and find out who she is and what her thoughts are.'

He does, noting the building entered by Fidele and the two ladies, and he vows to 'wait for the first opportunity'.

In the next entry, he's working in the home of the Director, sharpening quills in his office, when the daughter appears and drops her handkerchief. He picks it up and returns it to her, heart pounding, certain that she favours him. Two entries later, after his Chief berates him for his obvious interest in the Director's daughter when he's nothing but a lowly clerk, as opposed to Chief of Division like himself, the diarist decides to find out about the girl's private life by asking Madgie directly. When the dog perversely refuses to speak to him, he realizes he'll have to get her letters from Fidele.

In his next entry, for 12 November, he returns to the apartment of the two ladies, and when the younger of them asks what he wants:

'I want to have a talk with your doggie,' he says, interpreting her dumbfounded look as 'The girl was stupid.' Fidele tries to interfere, and as he reaches into the dog's basket she bites his leg, but to no avail, because he grabs the letters she's hidden under the straw. Gogol has the diarist report that at this point Fidele tries to be nice to him to win back the letters by kindness, but he's not fooled by this and he goes off, noting that 'I believe the girl mistook me for a madman – she seemed very frightened indeed.' The next day's entry presents the letters.

And what letters! The story line of the diarist's growing madness would have worked with letters of the simplest information, but Gogol's genius is to give us Madgie's correspondence as that of one young female to another; that is, not only does Gogol have the diarist believe he's reading the letters of a well-born, well-bred young lady who simply happens to be a dog, but he writes them in such detail that the readers get interested in them for their own sake, and Gogol almost makes you complicit in the diarist's insanity.

The first letter opens: 'Dear Fidele, I still find it difficult to get accustomed to the commonness of your name. Couldn't they find a better one for you? Fidele, like Rose, is very ordinary, but all that's beside the point. I'm very glad we have decided to write to each other.' The diarist breaks in here to observe that the spelling and punctuation is excellent, 'better than our Divisional Chief can do'.

And when, further in the letter, he reads 'I believe that sharing feelings and impressions with another is one of the main blessings in life…' his reaction is: 'Hm! The thought is stolen from a work translated from the German. The author's name escapes me now.' This is brilliant writing because it is so deeply delusional: the criticism of a letter written by a dog because it may be passing off some German Romanticism as her own thought! It's also your enjoyment of all this that involves you in the madness. After all, it's not surprising that the diarist, having invented these letters in his own mind, should both recognize the sentiment about sharing feelings and not quite remember the author he'd read who originally wrote the thought.

But what really excites the diarist is any mention in the letters of Madgie's mistress. When he reads 'My young mistress, whom her papa calls Sophie, is crazy about me,' he responds with 'Ouch! Never mind. Never mind. Silence!' which becomes his refrain every time his thoughts turn to Sophie, the daughter of the Director.

Madgie's letter (all imagined by the mad diarist, remember) moves into a lengthy description of the delicacies she gets to eat, and of the sort of food she doesn't like. It continues:

...What I hate is people who give dogs the little pellets they knead out of bread. Some person sitting at the table, who has previously touched all sorts of filthy things, begins to knead a piece of bread with those same hands, then calls you and thrusts the pellet into your mouth. It is awkward somehow to refuse and, disgusted, you eat it up...

By making his character's madness so interesting – a letter-writing dog who doesn't exist but whose non-existent letters are really amusing – you tend while reading to half believe in the craziness. It might delight the reader, but at this point the diarist breaks in with: 'What's that all about! What rubbish! As though there weren't more interesting things to write about. Let's see the next page. There may be something less stupid.' He, of course, is only interested in mentions of Sophie. That the diarist doesn't share your enjoyment makes it all the funnier. Gogol's method, even in creating a believable madman, is comedy.

When, finally, the letters reveal that the Director's daughter is in love with and soon to marry a guards' officer, the poor diarist is beside himself with disappointment, and he rips up the letter (which does not exist). In the next entry, still using reason, he argues that, since the girl obviously cannot marry him, a lowly clerk, perhaps he's not really a lowly clerk but actually someone important in disguise, like a general. Of course, the madman's logic leaves out the missing piece of the logical sequence – that she cannot marry him *but obviously wants to* – so much does he take it for granted. The subsequent entry has him ruminating over newspapers reporting the Spanish throne vacated and a search for an heir going on. He believes such an heir is around but has not yet made himself known. His next diary entry, for 8 December, has him puzzling this Spanish succession question all day.

The next entry is dated 'Year 2000, April 43'. He announces: 'This is a day of great jubilation. Spain has a king. They've found him. *I* am the King.' He first reveals this to his cleaning lady and records 'she flung up her hands in awe. She almost died of terror.' He interprets this as proof only that his newly discovered status is overpowering for the simple soul.

His royal delusion holds for almost the remainder of the story. He is able to interpret the madhouse he's taken to as the court of Spain; the lunatics with shaven heads as monks; the beatings he receives and the cold water dripped on his head as either the barbarity of Spanish custom, or a plot of the Inquisition or of foreign powers.

In the final entry, the diarist hasn't the strength to go on, and he drops all his mad rationale. He longs to fly away, he calls out to his dear mother to save him from this torture: 'Mother, take pity on your sick child…'

And then comes his last statement: 'And, by the way, have you heard that the Dey of Algiers has a wart right under his nose?'

It's as if Gogol lets you see the real suffering for a minute and then again curtains it with comedy. He can't leave you with the serious suffering since the entire story is, as so much else in Gogol, a satire on the insane stratification of Russian society in its vast civil service.

Key idea

Extreme or unusual dialogue is determined by the fiction you write and not merely by an idea of novelty.

If Gogol brings off the difficult feat of making you delight at the insane letters by a dog created in the head of a madman, about a century later, in 1929, William Faulkner brings off an even more amazing feat in his novel *The Sound and the Fury* by having its first part be literally a tale told by an idiot. Faulkner's great sleight of hand is to enable it to signify plenty. Its opening paragraph contains the central characteristics of Faulkner's method.

> Through the fence, between the curling flower spaces, I could see them hitting. They were coming toward where the flag was and I went along the fence. Luster was hunting in the grass by the flower tree. They took the flag out, and they were hitting. Then they put the flag back and they went to the table, and he hit and the other hit. Then they went on, and I went along the fence. Luster came away from the flower tree and we went along the fence and we stopped and I looked through the fence while Luster was hunting in the grass.

Impossibly, the idiot Benjamin speaks. Faulkner makes him speak very simply, but that he can in any way speak involves the suspension of your disbelief. Benjamin watches people 'hitting' and sees a 'flag' and sees 'They took the flag out', and by this time you understand the speaker is watching golf being played, and you're probably pleased to identify the 'table' as the tee just beside the green.

In the next two paragraphs Faulkner puts more demands on your ability to suspend your disbelief:

> 'Here, caddie.' He hit. They went across the pasture. I held to the fence and watched them going away.

'Listen at you, now.' Luster said. 'Ain't you something, thirty-three years old, going on that way. After I done went all the way to town to buy you that cake. Hush up that moaning. Ain't you going to help me find that quarter so I can go to the show tonight.'

The idiot who cannot speak and does not have language nor understand words can hear and report the language of others, not only that spoken to him, like Luster's speech, but that of a golfer speaking to his caddie. The next paragraph reveals that the idiot while he 'held to the fence' wasn't watching quietly. The idiot is able to tell you through Luster that he, Benjamin, has been 'moaning'. You will learn that moaning, with loud and louder bellowing, is one of his default sounds. The rest is silence. Further on you find that what has set off the moaning at the fence is the golfer saying 'Here, caddie,' because that's the sound of the name of Benjamin's long-gone, beloved sister Caddy. And naming the fairway 'the pasture' isn't Benjamin's special word but his memory of the pastureland it was before being sold off by his profligate father as a golf course, to raise money.

How does Faulkner manage this, having an idiot with perfect recall, able somehow to speak coherently? One important element of making us believe in Benjamin is that, emotionally, he is not an idiot. He is extremely sensitive to happiness and unhappiness, goodness and nastiness, in other people. And the other important element is you get very drawn in to Faulkner's way of having this idiot speak. It is, for instance, near metaphor when Benjamin refers to the flat green tee area as 'the table'. There's an intellectual and aesthetic fascination to this invented language that keeps you from thinking of dismissing the tale told by an idiot as literally an impossibility: you're too busy seeing and hearing the world through this limited consciousness.

Here, for example, in italicized flashback (Faulkner takes great care with clear visual presentation of shifts), is Benjamin speaking about being sent by his playboy uncle Maury with a letter to his mistress Mrs Patterson, whose husband suspects the affair:

Mr Patterson was chopping in the green flowers. He stopped chopping and looked at me. Mrs Patterson came across the garden, running. When I saw her eyes I began to cry. You idiot, Mrs Patterson said, I told him never to send you alone again. Give it to me. Quick. Mr Patterson came fast, with the hoe. Mrs Patterson leaned across the fence, reaching her hand. She was trying to climb the fence. Give it to me, she said, Give it to me. Mr Patterson climbed the fence. He took the letter. Mrs Patterson's dress was caught on the fence. I saw her eyes again and I ran down the hill.

The helplessness and clarity of the point of view are brilliant narrative devices. The fascination you feel as you read keeps you from seriously thinking about the literal impossibility of this character narrating. Faulkner can even have Mrs Patterson call Benjamin an idiot, which is what he is, without breaking the narrative spell.

Focus point

Extreme or unusual dialogue must hold your reader's attention; it must communicate, even if its means are unconventional.

Another technique Faulkner uses in the paragraph above is having two simpler statements rather than one slightly more complex statement. Benjamin first sees Mr Patterson 'chopping in the green flowers'. Then he sees Mr Patterson run 'with a hoe'. He doesn't say 'chopping with a hoe in the green flowers', although since he says 'chopping' and later 'hoe', Benjamin is just as capable of saying 'chopping with a hoe'. Faulkner writes 'chopping in the green flowers' because it is odder and cruder, especially the violent image of 'chopping' combined with the idiot's metaphor for weeds as 'green flowers'. Saying he saw Patterson 'chopping with a hoe' would definitely not be a tale told by this particular idiot, because his emotions extend to all living things, humans included, until humans turn nasty, like Mr Patterson, or too sad to bear, like Mrs Patterson. In fact, if Faulkner has a literary father figure for Benjamin, it's Dostoyevsky in *The Idiot*, which uses the Russian tradition of the holy fool.

Immediately after the flashback above, you find: '"They ain't nothing over yonder but houses," Luster said. "We going down the branch."' The idiot has looked to or even moved off towards the old Patterson house, but Luster knows nothing about that. Only Caddy might have guessed that, but she's not there, or only there for Benjamin as a loss, an echo in golf. Again, working out what Luster is referring to is part of the fascination of this stylized presentation.

Benjamin's tale is told on 7 April 1928, but his mind flips back to 23 December, perhaps in 1905, and back to 1913, when he did something or only was frightened by the girl's screams but he was anyway gelded. And in all these scenes you keep being reminded that he is an idiot, so, despite his perfect memory and sizeable vocabulary, you keep reading as if it wasn't being told by an idiot yet grateful that it is.

Key idea

Extreme or unusual dialogue can function to give insight about other aspects of your fiction, including its more conventional dialogue.

Write

No, you don't have to create an idiot or mad person. Think of characters you've created or are in the process of creating. Do any of them call for very unusual speech? What is it about them that might determine this? Make notes about what characteristics such speech might have.

So far in this chapter, you've seen examples of character-motivated extremes of dialogue. Faulkner's Benjamin is also there because Faulkner wanted a point of view that's purely motivated by emotional reaction – to good (kind) and to bad (mean) people, and to people who suffer.

Formal or structural motivation can also affect the nature of dialogue. The example given in the chapter's introduction was Georges Perec's novel written without using the letter *e*. But formal strictures need not be so extreme to produce special dialogue. Harry Mathews' novel *The Sinking of the Odradek Stadium* is written as an exchange of letters between a husband and wife, Zachary and Twang.

There are 103 letters sent to each other over the space of a year. Each of Zachary's letters contains a proper, the special prayer for that week of the Roman Catholic calendar. Each of Twang's letters includes an excerpt from a Buddhist meditational text. Though both characters write in English, Twang's first language is Pan (an invented language), and though Twang's English improves over the year, it's far from standard. These religious/philosophical demands are not the only constraints. On their own, they don't much alter the dialogue style in letter form. Zachary can begin a letter to Twang with 'Divine testimony is the best', but he follows with 'and your letters bristle with Eleusinian truths. By them I know I exist,' and he moves to 'even if I would rather you proved it by digging your nails into my palms, or your toe into my flank.'

And Twang is able to end one of her misspelled letters with the meditative:

> „,, So brothr, my mynd hargo of love seek you one-most in one deriction, then in a second derection, then in a 3rd derexion, then in a forth direction, like wise up ward, dwon ward, and all-round, the sence of to-love-like minde in-fusion all thing with no limit, no narrow, no to-hate, no ill desire.

Notice how the words themselves are shaped by the meanings, the different 'directions' of the spelling of 'direction' and the mixed numerical listing. And yet it appears a natural enough expression of her physical separation from her husband.

At the same time, another formal constraint is added. Twang's letters introduce and reintroduce words in Pan, like the closing salutation of the letter above: 'And I say, "Goodbye, *neng* of Twang."' Zachary's letters introduce conman's jargon, as in his letter quoted above when, in describing a museum visit he's made, he writes '"You shall be the two millionth visitor of our conchological collections," she [the beautiful guide] sweetly said to me, ending a vague hope that I might cop a heel.'

And, having slowly introduced the terms in Pan and conman's jargon to each other throughout the correspondence, they can, by letters 100 (C) and 101 (CI) trust that the other will understand letters entirely composed these ways.

C [Tang's letter to Zachary]

7 Pok Lai

Ru lemu! lemo vin mai uuax pristwi. Rhey mau neng, wey tharai duvai. Wuc Lao stheu atran, ticbai mai slop, nai: theu sheeno lai nob lucri nam aindap. (eels)

[The extract above does not include the special accent marks over vowels.]

To which Zachary replies:

CI

This chump never blowed you were turned out to hopscotch. You let him find the leather, and he copped you for the pure quill, when you're nothing but a crow. It took a long time to bobble him, but now you've knocked him good and he feels like a heavy gee had slipped him a shiv. Well, no twist will ever beat this savage again, not if she hands over her bottom bumblebee – it's cheaper loaning cush to Pogy O'Brien. Don't you play the hinge but stick to the big con. You're a class raggle with a grand future, even if this mark knows you're a snider.

If you've paid attention to the 99 previous letters, you'll get at least the gist of these two.

All in all, the combination of Pan, conman jargon, pidgin English (morning-dove English, perhaps), the propers for the Roman Catholic Mass and the Buddhist meditational texts helps construct a dialogue peculiar to this witty, comic treasure-and-pleasure hunt of a novel.

Key idea

Extreme or unusual dialogue can arise from formal conditions you impose on the language of your fiction.

Write

Just to see what happens to your dialogue and your interests, take a piece of dialogue you've written, either a single voice of one medium paragraph length, or a two-voice dialogue of about the same length – it can contain some identifying narrative – and do the following:

- Rewrite it without using the letter *u*.
- Rewrite it without using the letter *o*.
- Rewrite it without using the letter *i*.
- Rewrite it without using the letter *a*.
- Rewrite it without using the letter *e*.

One-sentence example:

> (original) Dialogue is strange when *e* is eliminated.

> (without *e*) Talk is odd without its most common non-consonant.

The final example is in some ways the strangest of all, since it involves no creation of any unusual dialogue. Margaret Laurence's 1964 novel *The Stone Angel* is a first-person narration of the speaker's life, much of it told in flashback from the memories of the 90-year-old Hagar Shipley. The novel is not formally experimental in the ordinary sense of the term. It is a novel of standard mid-twentieth-century realism.

What distinguishes Hagar's dialogue is that it reflects a particular point of view towards speech. The aged Hagar is no longer certain if she is actually saying something out loud or just thinking it. The only way she can find out with dignity is to look for any reaction from anyone who happens to be around her. You the reader can only know this in the same way, since you're reading first-person, present-tense narration (except for the flashbacks).

Hagar's son Marvin and his wife Doris live with Hagar in her big house, and the old woman reacts badly to Doris's suggestion she hire a nurse to help look after her. Then Doris makes another suggestion:

'We thought we'd go for a drive after supper,' Doris says. 'Would you like that?'

'Where to?'

'Oh, just out in the country.'

I nod, but my mind's not on it. I'm really thinking of the things not settled. How hard it is to concentrate on prime matters. Something is forever intruding. I've never had a moment to myself, that's been my trouble. Can God be One and watching? I see Him in immaculate radiance, a short white jacket and a smile white and creamy as zinc-oxide ointment, focusing his cosmic and comic glass eye on this and that, as the fancy takes Him. Or no – He's many-headed, and all the heads argue at once, a squabbling committee. But I can't concentrate, for I'm wondering really what barium is, and how it tastes, and if it'll make me sick.

'You'll come along, then?' Doris is saying.

'Eh? Come where?'

'For a drive. I said we thought we'd take a drive after supper.'

'Yes, yes. Of course I'll come. Why do you harp on it so? I said I'd come.'

'No, you never. I only wanted to make sure. Marv just hates plans to be changed at the last minute.'

'Oh, for mercy's sake. Nobody's changing plans. What're you talking about?'

She looks out the window and whispers to herself, thinking I can't hear.

'Prob'ly forget by supper, and we shan't go again.'

Is it that Hagar's attention has wandered? Is it that Doris hadn't seen her nod? Or is it the Hagar hadn't actually said 'Yes' to the original question? What you read here is not just the realistic vagaries of inattention in dialogue, but the loss of focus of an ageing brain. But the little exchange gains more significance when it turns out that the drive 'just out in the country' turns out to be a visit to a care home that Marvin and Doris hope Hagar will enter. None of Doris's anxiety can be explained during the scene because you follow it entirely through Hagar's immediate perceptions. And, as such, though well written, it doesn't contain any unusual concept of dialogue.

Hagar is so fearful of being stuck in a home with 'old people' (though she wonders how it can be she suddenly finds herself in a body so unresponsive and awkward to manage) that she decides to take matters into her own hands. The simplest social interactions are now sources of potential misunderstanding, as when she accompanies Doris to the local store.

> At the corner store a young girl is paying for a loaf of bread. She counts the money carefully. She's scarcely more than a child. I'm fascinated by her hands.
>
> 'Well, I never. Do you see her, Doris? She's wearing black nail polish. Black with specks of gilt. Really, I ask you – what's her mother thinking of, to allow it?'
>
> The child turns and stares malevolently, and I see from her face that she's considerably older than I thought.
>
> 'Oh, Mother –' Doris breathes into my ear. 'Can't you hush? Please, just for once –'
>
> How had it happened? I can't face Doris or the black-fingered girl or anyone. Oh, I'll speak no more, ever, to a living soul. Until my last breath I'll hold my wayward tongue. I won't, though – that's the trouble.

Her perceptions have become socially archaic. And perhaps she doesn't see so well, mistaking a young woman for a girl. And maybe she's forgotten to voice such observations in a whisper. For certain these are problems of the old.

She finally gets the chance to put her escape plan into action on a day when Marvin is out to work and Doris has gone shopping. She takes her old-age pension cheque, cashes it at the bank, takes the local bus to the downtown depot, gets help there from a girl to find the ticket window and get onto the correct bus to take her to a place she remembers at the ocean. When she gets off the bus at a service station, she sees a small store attached and goes in and buys provisions. The woman at the counter says:

> 'That be all now? That's three fifty-nine.'
>
> So much for these few things?
>
> Then I see from her frown that a terrible thing has occurred. I've spoken the words aloud.
>
> 'The bars are twenty-five apiece,' she says coldly. 'Did you want the ten-cent ones?'
>
> 'No, no,' I can't get the words out fast enough. 'It's quite all right.

I only meant – everything's so high these days, isn't it?'

'It's high all right,' she says in a surly voice, 'but it's not us that gains, in the smaller stores. It's the middlemen, and that's for sure, sitting on their fannies and not doing a blame thing except raking in the dough.'

'Oh yes, I'm sure you're right.'

In fact, I haven't the foggiest notion what she's talking about. I hate my breathless agreement, but I've no choice. I mouth effusive thanks, unable to stop myself.

The statement 'So much for these few things?' is presented without quotation marks so you first take it, as Hagar does, for a thought, and then, with her, you understand from the storekeeper's reaction that she's spoken it. This is a simple but striking innovation – removing the boundaries between thought and dialogue – and it marks yet a further stage in the slow disintegration of Hagar's mind.

No sooner does Hagar leave the store when she hears the door jingle open and the woman appears. 'You forgot your parcel,' she says, accusingly. 'Here.' Hagar then sees a sign with an arrow saying *To the Point*. A truck draws up and the driver offers her a ride. When she says she's going to the Point, he tells her it's lucky he came by: it's three miles away. The world is now strange to her: she hasn't been shopping so she doesn't know the prices; she hasn't travelled on her own so she doesn't know the distances. Still, with luck and great will power and more energy than she imagined she had, Hagar gets out of the truck and makes it through the woods, stopping to rest and falling asleep on a log, and she even manages to get down the long flight of cliff steps and onto the beach by the old disused fish cannery. There, greatly exhausted, she takes shelter in the old cannery manager's house. She eats some of the provisions she's bought and falls into a series of naps and memories, many of them about her beloved son John, who died after a truck accident while drunk. A man then turns up in the derelict house and frightens her. But it turns out he's a very ordinary man who at times just comes out there to get away and spend the night drinking some wine. Once Hagar understands he's a decent person, she feels reassured. They share food and wine and she falls asleep.

During the night there occurs one of Hagar's longest flashbacks, to the last year of John's life, when he had at last found a good woman who cared for him and helped him to stop drinking. The memories of his final days, the accident that killed his woman and John's subsequent death in hospital as Hagar watched at his bedside are harrowing. At their end, you read this:

I'm crying now, I think. I put a hand to my face, and find the skin slippery with my tears. Then, startlingly, a voice speaks beside me.

'Gee, that's too bad.'

I can't think who it is, and then I recall – a man was here, and we talked, and I drank his wine. But I didn't mean to tell him all this.

'Have I been saying it all aloud?'

'It's okay,' he says. It's quite okay. Do you good to tell it.'

Laurence uses this technique of doing away with the separation between thought and dialogue not merely to create the 'realistic' experience of the mind's disintegration in extreme old age – though that itself is fascinating – but in this great scene to show Hagar that her lifetime of proud silence has been a destructive vanity for those who meant most to her. She has never before spoken of her deep regrets, not acknowledged to anyone the mistakes she knows she's made until now, unwittingly, and she is aware of what a waste of life her cruel pride has been.

There may well be other uses of this blurring the boundary between thought and speech in fiction. But Margaret Laurence makes the technique her own in this novel's development with intense implications for character insight in the service of psychological realism.

Focus point

Extreme or unusual dialogue can result from eliminating the distinctions between thought and speech, and between narrative and dialogue. You should have more than an arbitrary reason for removing these boundaries.

 ## Write

Think of situations other than the debilitating effect of age which could produce this effect of confusion between thought and dialogue. Might you want to use the technique?

Focus points

This chapter has looked at extremely unusual forms of dialogue. Its main ideas are summarized in the following five points.

- Extreme and/or unusual forms of dialogue must be justified by the demands of your particular fiction.
- Extreme/unusual dialogue can arise from who a particular character is. The character can be 'different' in speech for a variety of social, physical or psychological reasons.
- Extreme/unusual dialogue can be prompted by the setting of your fiction. This may be archaic (fantasy) or futuristic (fantasy/science fiction) or determined by any number of demands on language by the societal construction of such imagined worlds.
- Extreme/unusual dialogue can arise from structural considerations, such as the writer's desire to have an 'outside' or more 'objective' view of the fictional characters and events. Such dialogue may also arise from a variety of formal constraints put on the language.
- Extreme or unusual dialogue can result from the author's blurring or doing away with the boundaries between thought and speech. With first-person narration, this may also mean the disintegration of boundaries between narrative and dialogue.

Next step

The next chapter, the final chapter, looks at the important art in dialogue of not listening. It also presents several ways you can learn about your fiction from your characters themselves.

10

The art of not listening; learning from listening

In this chapter you will learn:

- About the various reasons for 'not listening' in dialogue
- That 'not listening' in dialogue is an important tool in characterization and plotting
- How 'listening' to your characters' dialogue can give you a deeper understanding of them.

Back in Chapter 1, dialogue from Richard Russo's *Empire Falls* was excerpted as an example of getting a character's specific language just right. But it's a good example of something else, so here it is again:

'I could use the extra scratch,' Max said, following in step and causing Miles to make a mental note to keep an eye on him tonight. His father hated work but loved crowds, probably because chaos created more opportunities than order.

'Put on a clean shirt before you go out front,' Miles reminded him.

'I've worked here before, you know.'

'And an apron,' Miles said. And wash your hands.'

'Wash my hands so I can bus dirty dishes?'

Miles, the restaurant manager, has not responded to Max's comment about having worked at the restaurant not because he hasn't heard the comment but because he knows his intelligent bum of a father needs to hear these basic rules repeated, and because responding to Max's comment would probably get him involved in a long meander of conversation whose end result would be for Max an enjoyable argument and for him a waste of half an hour in a very busy day.

Russo knows the dialogue art of 'not listening' very well. This version of not listening is simply having one character ignore part of the dialogue of another.

What are the varieties of 'not listening' in dialogue?

The example above could be thought of as conscious ignoring or avoidance. The listener has actually heard what's been said but has reason not to respond.

Another variety could be called the deafness of deception. The listener has heard what's been said, but acknowledging it would force a response of either a direct lie or the admission of a truth which would end the deception and cause problems. The earlier example from *Nightmare Abbey* when the son, rather than have to answer his father's question about whether he's hidden a girl somewhere around the room, pretends he hasn't heard and, to his father's louder and louder repetition of the question, keeps giving a louder and louder lecture on the anatomy of the ear, which he's doing his best not to use. This is an extreme of farce, but you can imagine any number of more realistic instances.

For instance, George, whose car is being repaired, has borrowed his wife Jenny's car to attend a business meeting 'which will run late', he's told her. There actually was a business meeting, but what ran late was the monkey-business meeting with his girlfriend Georgia afterwards. And George stupidly then loaned Georgia the car. Now it's the next day, Saturday morning.

Jenny came back in by the kitchen door. 'George? Where's my car?'

He lifted his face from the coffee mug. 'I can't tell you what an endless mess that meeting was last night.'

'Good, because I don't want to know. Where's the car?'

'I thought it would be over by nine, ten at the latest, and –'

'George, you just said you can't tell me. So don't. Instead, tell me where the car is. My car?'

'It must have been after midnight, closer to one.'

'Where have you parked my car?'

'By the time –'

'Oh, my God: you've crashed my car, haven't you?'

'Absolutely not. Absolutely. No.'

'Then where is it? I have to pick up Toby in fifteen minutes.'

'I'm trying to tell you. It was so late, and Clumpers, old Rob Harrison –'

'Toby. You remember Toby, our son, George?'

'Of course. Why should I forget my son? I mean, he's our only child. It's not like we have dozens of children under foot.'

George hears very well. He picks up anything Jenny says to postpone answering, while working out the lie to tell her.

Another reason for not hearing can be the listener's certainty that what is being said cannot be true, cannot have happened, cannot be possible. This might be called the deafness of faith, or of vanity.

You could imagine a scene in which someone who's applied for a prestigious position – say, an academic, a lecturer who's applied for a professorship in the same department – being called in to meet with the chair of the search committee at about the time the decision is due. So sure is the lecturer that the job is his – he might be the only in-house candidate, he might be particularly friendly with this committee chair and the department chair, etc. – that he cannot hear that he's being told he has not been successful. He might take certain signals the wrong way, like the chair saying she wanted to speak first with him as they're friends, or the chair might begin by saying the lecturer knows that he was her own choice through the selection process. Such a dialogue can be written so that every time the chair believes she's telling him 'by letting him down lightly', the listening lecturer interprets this as another sign of his success. It can be structured so that even when the chair is forced to tell him he hasn't been selected, even when she tells him who has been selected, he manages to misinterpret this according to his 'faith' or his ego, or his trust in the old boy network, etc.

Not listening may also be due to the listener focusing on those parts of what the other says that are of much more interest or importance to her/him and switching off at other topics. This is, of course, selective inattention or selective deafness.

Physical deafness itself may be a cause of not hearing, but you, like the rest of us, probably know examples of someone hard of hearing able to hear some things as opposed to others as a function of interest. This is more literally selective deafness.

A character may be really very deaf, but this type of 'not listening' is clearly not a function of character or relationship with the speaker. As a writer, you need to remember this. It can be a factor in plotting, but it has nothing to do with the art or craftiness of not listening.

Other factors in not listening may involve genuine misunderstanding due to not understanding the meaning of words or expressions or particular jargon. It would be possible, for example, for a certain type of adult to speak to a four-year-old child in a diction essentially inaccessible for the child ('essentially inaccessible' would be a way of telling the child not to go under the dining table bound to fail).

Some dialogue in fiction involves non-verbal aspects which produce a failure to listen to specific content. The speaker may be weeping, for instance, which not only makes understanding the words more difficult but can inhibit verbal understanding because of emotional distraction in the listener – from deep empathy to strong revulsion. Facial expression and body language can also play inhibiting roles in listening.

There may also be mixed signals: the jolly way the doctor tells the patient the test results were positive, in which the word 'positive' itself might momentarily confuse the patient into thinking positive means 'good'.

Finally, character assumptions of behaviour can also lead to not listening. The most infamous of these is the man, typically, who 'hears' his date's 'No! Don't!' as 'Yes! Do!' Sexual, racial, ethnic and age stereotyping are also (too) commonly causes of not listening. You, the writer, also need to be aware of these possibilities.

How do you learn about your own characters from listening to their dialogue?

When I'm having difficulties understanding my characters in enough
depth, I've found two techniques useful. The first is bringing them
together for a personal talk. This talk may never occur in the story
or novel. Its primary purpose is to let them literally tell me more
about themselves than I knew before.

I discovered this technique accidentally. I had two characters in a
work relationship. Both had started together, but, though they'd
both been promoted, one, Tom, had ended up in a considerably more
senior position than the other, Lenny, who had badly compromised
his status some years earlier. I was writing a scene in which Tom

phones Lenny to say he's in his home neighbourhood and is thinking of dropping over. My plan was for a short scene of dialogue in which Tom gives Lenny some work-related information of a private nature and then leaves. Instead, I found, once they were face to face, they just talked and talked about various family problems, told bad jokes, and were, at one level, wasting my time. But I kept writing and they kept yakking. Twenty-five manuscript pages later, hand aching, I managed to stop. I certainly had written the characters enough before this to be able to hear their voices as they spoke, and as I wrote I didn't worry about narrative. I was just writing and listening. At the end, I knew much more about each character and much more about their relationship, past and present, than I had at the start. No more than two or three of these 25 pages made it into the novel, but it was an invaluable afternoon's work. It gave me a wider and deeper understanding of these important characters.

 Key idea

> You may be able to learn more about your characters by bringing them together and letting them talk, even if such dialogue scenes won't appear in what you're writing.

My other discovery was after the fact. I noticed, halfway through a draft of a novel, that a woman character had really come to life during a serious argument with her husband. When I looked back over her earlier experiences, I found I could use what 'she' had revealed in that argument scene to rewrite her as a more complex and more interesting character. Since then, I've on occasion used the argument technique to learn from my characters about my characters, even though few of these exercise arguments come into the finished fiction.

 Key idea

> You may discover more about characters by writing a scene of dialogue argument, even if it remains only an exercise.

Focus point

The 'learning from argument technique' can be especially useful for types of characters you know give you difficulty; for example women characters, old people, or shy and introspective people.

Write

Use the conversation or argument technique to write dialogue for one of your characters about whom you want to know more and/ or to have a deeper understanding.

Focus points

The main ideas of this chapter are summarized in the following five points:

- Writing good dialogue involves being aware that people, characters, often don't listen to each other for a variety of reasons.
- Not listening in dialogue scenes can be a potent means of characterization.
- Not listening can also be a significant plot mechanism.
- Bringing your characters together to talk could be an exercise that enables you to learn more, and in more depth, about your characters, whether or not any of the exercise makes it into your fiction.
- Another useful exercise, especially for types of characters you find you have trouble making credible and interesting, is to write a scene of argument in dialogue.

Next Step

Keep writing, keep reading, keep listening. Keep writing.

References

Chapter 1

Elias Canetti, *Auto Da Fé (Die Blendung)*, Penguin Books, 1946, trans. C.V. Wedgwood and Elias Canetti

Richard Russo, *Empire Falls*, Vintage, 2002

Chapter 2

Bernice Rubens, *Madame Sousatzka*, Eyre & Spottiswoode, 1962

Louise Erdrich, *Love Medicine*, Harper Perennial, 1993

J.D. Salinger, 'For Esmé with Love and Squalor', in *Nine Stories*, Little, Brown and Company, 1953

J.D. Salinger, *The Catcher in the Rye*, Little, Brown and Company, 1951

Frank O'Connor, 'Soirée Chez une Belle Jeune Fille', in *My Oedipus Complex and Other Stories*, Penguin Modern Classics, 2005

Chapter 3

Mary Robison, 'Pretty Ice', in *Days*, Alfred A. Knopf, 1979

Cormac McCarthy, *All the Pretty Horses*, Alfred A. Knopf, 1992

William Trevor, 'Men of Ireland', in *Selected Stories*, Penguin Books, 2010

Henry James, *Washington Square*, Bantam Classics, 1959

Chapter 4

Ali Smith, *Girl Meets Boy*, Canongate, 2007

Irving Weinman, *Stealing Home*, John Daniel, 2004

Ian McEwan, *On Chesil Beach*, Jonathan Cape, 2007

Julian Barnes, *The Sense of an Ending*, Jonathan Cape, 2011

Chapter 5

Samuel Richardson, *Pamela*, Chapman & Hall, 1902

Daniel Defoe, *Moll Flanders*, Peter Davies, 1929

Daniel Defoe, *A Journal of the Plague Year*, Routledge, 1884

A.S. Byatt, *Possession*, Chatto & Windus, 1990

Irving Weinman, *Wolf Tones*, John Daniel, 2009

Chapter 6

Angela Carter, 'Black Venus's Tale', Next Editions, 1980

Richard Russo, *Empire Falls*, Vintage, 2002

Chapter 7

Thomas Love Peacock, *Nightmare Abbey*, vol. 1 in *The Novels of Thomas Love Peacock*, Hart-Davies, MacGibbon, 1977

Ann Beattie, 'The Burning House', in *Park City: New and Selected Stories*, Alfred A. Knopf, 1998

Fyodor Dostoyevsky, *Crime and Punishment*, Harper, 1951, trans. Constance Garnett

Charles Dickens, *Barnaby Rudge*, Hazell, Watson & Viney Ltd. (printed from 1867–68 edition)

Chapter 8

Willa Cather, *Death Comes for the Archbishop*, Heinemann, 1927

Cormac McCarthy, *All the Pretty Horses*, Alfred A. Knopf, 1992

Ernest Hemingway, *The Short Stories of Ernest Hemingway*, The Modern Library, 1938

Irving Weinman, *Wolf Tones*, John Daniel, 2009

Irving Weinman, *Virgil's Ghost*, Ballantine, 1990

Mona Simpson, *My Hollywood*, Alfred A. Knopf, 2010

James Berry, *A Thief in the Village*, Hamish Hamilton, 1987

D.H. Lawrence, *Lady Chatterley's Lover*, Penguin, 1967

Peter Matthiessen, *Far Tortuga*, Vintage Books, 1988

Toni Morrison, *Jazz*, Chatto & Windus, 1992

Monica Ali, *Brick Lane*, Doubleday, 2003

Chapter 9

Nikolai Gogol, *The Diary of a Madman and Other Stories*, Signet, 1969, trans. Andrew R. MacAndrew

William Faulkner, *The Sound and the Fury*, Modern Library, 1946

Harry Mathews, *The Sinking of the Odradek Stadium*, Dalky Archive Press, 1999

Margaret Laurence, *The Stone Angel*, Virago, 1986

Chapter 10

Richard Russo, *Empire Falls*, Vintage, 2002

Index